HAS AMERICA GONE TOO FAR?

BY:
DR. DON LEDBETTER

XULON PRESS

Xulon Press
2301 Lucien Way #415
Maitland, FL 32751
407.339.4217
www.xulonpress.com

© 2019 by Dr. Don Ledbetter

All rights reserved solely by the author. The author guarantees all contents are original and do not infringe upon the legal rights of any other person or work. No part of this book may be reproduced in any form without the permission of the author. The views expressed in this book are not necessarily those of the publisher.

Scripture quotations taken from the King James Version (KJV)–*public domain.*

Printed in the United States of America.

ISBN-13: 9781545661376

Contents

Introduction xi
Chapter 1: Where is America spiritually? 1
Satan's influence upon America 1
Satan's influence in America's social agenda 3
Satan's influence has permeated politics 5
Satan's influence has permeated Political Departments 6
    The IRS scandal 6
    The GSA Scandal 6
    The Benghazi Scandal 6
    The Obamacare Scandal 7
    The Clinton Emails Scandal 7
    Fast and Furious Scandal 10
    The Solyndra Scandal 10
    The Selling of Uranium to Russia Scandal 11
Satan uses the Media to advance his Agenda 12
Satan uses protest 13
Satan uses Religious scandals 15
    Ted Haggard 16
    Jim Baker 16
    John Geoghan 16
    Paul R. Shanley 17
    Sheikh Omar Abdel-Rahman: 17
    Jimmy Swaggart 17
Satan uses the Confederate flag and statues 18
Satan masquerades as an Angel of light 19
Attacks against Christianity 21
Is America on the verge of revival? 23

What relevance does the second coming of Christ have
on God's judgment on America?.................... 27
Will America undergo judgment before The
Second Coming?...................................31
Chapter 2: God Judged Judah...................... 32
The background for Jeremiah's ministry.............. 33
    Judah no longer believed God was sovereign....... 33
    The leadership of Judah had forsaken God......... 35
    King Hezekiah................................. 37
    King Manasseh 39
    King Amon 43
    King Josiah.................................... 44
    King Jehoahaz................................. 48
    King Jehoiakim 48
    King Jehoiachin 51
    King Zedekiah................................. 53
The spiritual leadership of Judah had Forsaken God...... 56
Jeremiah was a faithful servant...................... 57
The People of Judah were guilty of forsaking God 66
The people of Judah were guilty of Forsaking
God's Covenants 67
What did God say would happen if His people
failed to keep His covenants?....................... 69
The People of Judah had forsaken God in their
family life... 73
The People of Judah had forsaken God in
their worship 76
God rejected the people of Judah's religious
Practices... 77
What was Jeremiah's message? 81
God judges Judah 84
Jeremiah mourns over his Nation 90
Chapter 3: Has America Gone Too Far?............. 94
America's political leadership has forsaken God 97

President Richard Nixon: 99
President Gerald Ford: 99
President Jimmy Carter: 100
President Ronald Reagan: 101
President Bill Clinton: 102
President George W. Bush 104
President Barack Hussein Obama: 105
Who controls America? 107
Spiritual leaders have forsaken God 111
God is forsaken in our homes 115
Does it matter how we live? 116
God is forsaken in schools 117
God is forsaken in churches 122
God is forsaken by False Preachers 125
Americans deny personal sin 127
Chapter 4: Preparing for God's judgment 130
The Coming of Christ 130
The coming of the antichrist 136
The Antichrist and the False Prophet 137
Dangerous times are coming 142
What should the non-Christian do? 143
What should the Christian do? 146
What is the proof God will Judge America? 151
When Will God Judge America? 151
    Hurricanes 152
    Tornados 153
    Drugs 154
    Wild Fires 154
    Gangs 156
    Unknown Events 157
Footnotes 159
Who is Don Ledbetter? 173

Introduction

America, and the world, has become accustomed to sin. The message of the church, calling for Godly living, is all but silent. Messages on the doctrine of judgment and the reality of hell are rare. While the world slips further into sin, the church has become an entertainment center. The plan of Satan is to create a world so void of the presence of God, and His righteousness, the people of the world will cry out for a ruler to bring about a peaceful solution to the world's problems. We are hearing calls for a world leader today. When one considers the condition of the world and the church, it is not difficult to believe Satan is successful at what he is doing.

The Bible reveals, in Matthew 24:32-34, the parable of the fig tree. Many believe this parable is a reference to the rebirth of Israel, which occurred in 1948. If this is an accurate interpretation of this parable, then, what Jesus said about this parable places us on the verge of His return. The time just before the return of Christ will be a time of spiritual depravity. Paul tells us in II Thessalonians 2:1-3, "Let no man deceive you by any means: for that day shall not come, except there come a falling away first, and that man of sin be revealed, the son of perdition." Daniel, chapter 8, informs us this "man of sin," the "Antichrist," will become the leader of a One World Government. We are hearing politicians calling for "globalism." This is just another name for a One World Government.

Most Americans are spiritually ignorant of Satan's plan to lead the world to accept the rule of the Antichrist. Paul tells us in II Corinthians 4:4, Satan has blinded the minds of nonbelievers, preventing them from seeing and understanding the truths of God's Word. As America becomes more and more spiritually depraved, messages from pulpits across America make one wonder if America's pastors are aware of the dangers that exist. Evidence indicates most spiritual leaders have a greater desire to appease their congregations than to please God. Many pastors exhibit a paralyzing fear that prevents them from sharing the truth of God's Word against social and political issues the Bible condemns. Jeremiah said his nation failed because of the sins of the prophets and the iniquities of the priest of his day (Lamentations 4:13). Jeremiah's messages also condemned the political and spiritual leadership of his day.

God called Jeremiah to share His message to a sinful nation. Judah had forsaken God. Though the people of Judah acknowledged God, they refused to believe they were sinful and were angry when Jeremiah accused them of their sinfulness. They saw no reason to repent, nor would they accept Jeremiah's message God would judge them. For forty years, Jeremiah proclaimed God's message of his nation's sinfulness and God's call to repentance. He was beaten, publically ridiculed, imprisoned, and threatened with death because of the truths he shared.

The political leadership of Judah demonstrates they were unconcerned about the spiritual condition of their nation. They lived for self. This is true of most of the political leadership of America. Since the election of Donald Trump, America is becoming aware of the corruption that permeates America's political society. Our government leaders have established a two-tiered judicial system. Washington politicians have exempted themselves from many of the laws they establish for Americans. We are learning how top officials of the FBI, the CIA, the DEA, the IRS, and the Justice Department have violated the rights of the American people. The Secretary of State, the Attorney General, and others under the Obama Administration, misled Congress and the American people to cover their crimes. It would appear that each of the unlawful acts of these individuals occurred with complete disregard for the law. The question of many Americans is, "Will they ever be charged?"

Most Americans willingly admit they are sinners. Yet, very few give evidence they have a biblical understanding of the consequences of unforgiven sin. Today, the opinion of many is that you can believe what you want, live as you please, and believe when you die, you will go to heaven. As popular as this view may be, it is not biblical. When you consider only twenty-four percent of Americans believe the Bible is the literal Word of God, one can understand why so many accept ungodly social issues. Evidence indicates most Americas do not believe the sinfulness of America deserves God's judgment. Americans, like the people of Judah, believe God loves too much to judge their nation.

For forty years, Jeremiah pled with the political leaders, the spiritual leaders, and the people of Judah to repent and return to God. He warned them of the consequences if they refused God's commands. They denied their sinfulness and refused to accept that God would judge them. Is it not reasonable to believe, if God judged the people of Judah for the same sins American's are committing, He will also judge America? Judah had digressed to such a spiritual state, God declared them incurable (II Chronicles 36:16). America has become as sinful as Judah. Judah sacrificed their children by burning them to a false god, Baal (Jeremiah 19:5). Americans sacrifice their children to the god of convenience---abortion. Judah exchanged their worship of God to the worship of idols made with their own hands. Americans have exchanged their worship of God to the worship of the idols of entertainment and self-gratification. Judah refused to accept God's messengers who shared with them the Truth. Americans have done the same. Despite the clear evidence of Judah's sinfulness, the people of Judah refused to believe they needed to repent. Despite the clear evidence of America's sinfulness, most Americans refuse to believe they need to repent.

The purpose of this book is twofold. First, it is to show a parallel between the nation of Judah during the days of Jeremiah and America, today. In II Chronicles 36:11-21, there is a synopsis of the times of Jeremiah. These verses reveal Judah became spiritually depraved, and God declared them incurable. This is the spiritual condition of America today. Then, as now, there is a reluctance for individuals to admit the depth of their sinfulness, or that God will judge sinful people or a sinful nation. The people of America need to hear what God asked Jeremiah to do concerning Judah, as found in Jeremiah 5:1-9. God instructed Jeremiah:

> Run ye to and fro through the streets of Jerusalem and see now, and know, and seek in the broad places thereof, if ye can find a man, if there be any that executeth judgments, that seeketh the truth; and I will pardon it. And though they say, The Lord liveth, surely they swear falsely. O Lord, are not thine eyes upon the truth? Thou has striken them, but they have not grieved: thou has consumed them, but they have refused to receive correction: they have made their faces harder than a rock: they have refused to return. Therefore, I said, surely, these are poor; they are foolish: for they know not the way of the

Lord, nor the judgment of their God. I will get me unto the great men and will speak unto them: for they have known not the way of the Lord, and the judgment of their God: but these have altogether broken the yoke and burst the bonds. Wherefore a lion out of the forest shall slay them, and a wolf of the evenings shall spoil them, a leopard shall watch over their cities: every one that goeth out thence shall be torn in pieces: because their transgressions are many and their backslidings are increased. How shall I pardon thee for this? Thy children have forsaken me, and swore by them that are no gods: when I had fed them to the full they then committed adultery, and assembled themselves by troops in the harlots' house. They were as fed horses in the morning every one neighed after his neighbor's wife. Shall I not visit for these things? saith the Lord: and shall not my soul be avenged on such a nation as this?

The second purpose for this book is to sound a warning of God's impending judgment on America. Jeremiah's day was a day when sin was prevalent; when most who lived in Judah refused to believe they were sinful and deserved God's judgment. So it is today in America. The message of most preachers in Judah failed to proclaim God's requirements for His people. Preachers failed to confront sin and preached God loved too much to judge. This is the message of many preachers today.

As you consider the moral, social, and spiritual changes taking place in America, ask yourself, "If God judged Judah for the same sins America is committing, will He not also judge

America?" A greater question you should ask yourself is, "Am I ready for God's judgment?"

This book contains four chapters.

- Chapter 1 reveals the spiritual depravity of America.
- Chapter 2 illustrates the sinfulness of Judah and the reasons God judged Judah.
- Chapter 3 asks the question, "Has America Gone Too Far?"
- Chapter 4 seeks to help the reader prepare for the judgment that is to come.

Chapter 1

WHERE IS AMERICA SPIRITUALLY?

Satan's influence upon America

Most Americans would acknowledge that America has problems. Some would say, "America's problems are social." Many others would say, "America's problem is sin." When the statement is made, "America is no longer a Christian Nation," many are offended. (1) However, the facts speak for themselves. Only 24% of Americans believe the Bible is the literal word of God. The absence of America's spiritual interest is reflective in the fact that church attendance, financial giving through the local church, and concern for the lost and unchurched Christians are all in decline. Religious verbiage and dreaming does not change the fact that America suffers from the same spiritual depravity that the nation of Judah experienced during the days of Jeremiah.

For over two hundred years, America has stood as a beacon of God's grace and mercy to the world. Americans have given their lives through their service, and by their blood, to promote freedom for nationalities of people who despise our generous spirit. The people of America have published and promoted the gospel around the world through printed material and through the sacrifice of spirit-filled missionaries and laypersons. Because of Americans' belief in God, and efforts to evangelize the world for Christ, Satan has made America the central target of his attacks. As we approach the coming of Christ, Satan is doing his best to silence America's spiritual influence. The spiritual condition of America reveals Satan is accomplishing his objective.

Is Satan real? Who is the source behind all the evil that is taking place throughout our world? Some are of the opinion, these evil events just occur by happenchance. The Bible reveals Satan is real. Can we trust the Bible? This question demands an answer before one places their trust in biblical teachings. The Bible is unarguably the bestselling, most quoted, most published, most circulated, most translated, and most influential book in the history of humankind. Why is this so? It is so because there is no other book like the Bible. The Bible deals with issues that are relevant to everyone. Its truths have withstood every allegation and assault.

As one examines the Bible, they will discover the Bible declares Satan is real and a powerful force that opposes God, Christians, the Church, and all who seek to prevent the world from embracing God's redemptive plan for mankind. The Bible presents Satan as a brilliant strategist who lurks in the shadows, working his plans through acts of deception. The Bible further describes Satan as a liar, an accuser, a deceiver, a destroyer, and one who seeks to rule the lives of all humanity.

We need to understand that we are at war with, and under attack from, Satan. It is not by accident Satan lurks in the shadows. He knows, if he can distort man's view of who he is or prevent humanity from accepting the fact he truly exists, his attacks will be more effective. Understanding who our enemy is and how he operates, allows us to prepare for his attacks, putting us on the offensive rather than on the defensive. John tells us in Revelation 12:9; Satan will deceive the whole world. Christ tells us in the last days, there will be false Christs and false prophets that will produce great signs and wonders in an attempt to deceive (Matthew 24:24).

How is Satan accomplishing his attacks against America? Satan attacks the mind. He attacks one's mind with lies, half-truths, distortions, gimmicks, and schemes. His distortion is to prevent or to destroy man's understanding of God or man's relationship with God. Jesus tells us in John 10:10, "Satan has come to steal, and to kill, and to destroy." Peter tells us in I Peter 5:8, "Be sober, (clearheaded) be vigilant; (watchful) because your adversary the devil, as a roaring lion, walketh about, seeking whom he may devour." He is a master of deception and manipulation. He has an uncanny ability to transform himself into whatever, and to use whomever, he deems necessary to accomplish his objective. In John 8:44, Satan is a liar and the Father of lies. He attacks truth with lies and half-truths to create doubt. He uses doubt to divide. He uses doubt and division to destroy. Satan has Americans living in a perpetual state of doubt. Like Judah, in the days of Jeremiah, America is in serious trouble. If you doubt this, consider the following.

Satan's influence in America's social agenda

Satan's influence affects America's social agenda. Across America on any given day, upward of thirty-five-hundred unborn babies die by abortion. Since the Supreme Court legalized abortion in the landmark case of Roe versus Wade in 1973, upward of sixty million babies have been aborted. (2) Selling the body parts of these aborted babies has become a very lucrative profession. Satan has convinced those in the abortion industry that what they are doing is not wrong.

More than four decades after the U.S. Supreme Court's Roe v. Wade decision, opponents and supporters of abortion rights are still battling over this issue in the court room, at the ballot box, and in state legislatures. Many view abortion as a repugnant act of cruelty. Satan uses abortion as a means to divide America. The Psalmist speaks of sacrificing the blood of innocent children in Psalms 106:37-38, "They sacrificed their sons and their daughters to false gods. They shed innocent blood, the blood of their sons and daughters, whom they sacrificed to the idols of Canaan." The murder of these children angered the Lord. God is no less angry at America for the shedding of the blood of aborted babies.

Satan's influence has invaded the sanctity of marriage. He has created doubt and divided the opinion of many concerning the legalization of same sex marriages. Christians and others who accept the biblical concept of what constitutes a biblical marriage will remember June 26, 2015 as a sad day. Five of the Justices of the Supreme Court rejected the opinion of the majority of Americans, and thousands of years of social and religious acceptance and legalized same sex marriages. Justice Anthony Kennedy, who wrote the majority opinion, said, "It would misunderstand these men and women to say they disrespect the idea of marriage. There plea is that they do respect it, respect it so deeply that they seek to find its fulfillment for themselves." His words do not legitimize a sin so heinous that God says it is an abomination, (Leviticus 19:21-22; 20:13; Romans1:27). In a strongly worded decent, Judge Antonia Scalia said, "Today's decree says that my Ruler, and the Ruler of 320 Million Americans coast-to-cost, is a majority of nine lawyers on the Supreme Court." He also said, "The Supreme Court's ruling in favor of gay marriage shows just how much trouble America democracy is in." In both statements, he was right.

Satan's influence has permeated politics

Most Americans hold politicians in low esteem. On September 14, 2010, former Hartford, Connecticut mayor, Eddie Perez, a Democrat, was sentenced to eight years in prison on five corruption charges. On March 5, 2010, former Birmingham, Alabama mayor, Larry Langford, a Democrat, was sentenced to 15 years in prison for conspiracy, bribery and fraud, money laundering, and filing false tax returns. On October 12, 2005, Frank Ballance, a Democrat-congressman from North, Carolina, was sentenced to four years in prison for conspiring to defraud taxpayers. On November 28, 2005, Duke Cunningham, a former Republican-congressman from California, pleaded guilty to charges of conspiracy to commit bribery, mail fraud, wire fraud, and tax evasion.(3) On June 29, 2006, former Alabama governor, Don Siegelman, a Democrat, was found guilty of bribery, mail fraud, and obstruction of justice. On September 6, 2006, George H. Ryan, former governor of Illinois, a Republican, was sentenced to prison on fraud and racketeering charges. On June 11, 2007, Larry Craig, former Idaho Republican senator, was arrested for "lewd conduct" in a public restroom. (4) On November 13, 2009, former politician, William Jefferson, a Democrat-congressman from Louisiana, was convicted of 11 counts of bribery and sentenced to 13 years in prison. These are but a few of the many politicians who have violated their oath of office and been convicted of crimes in a court of law. (5)

Satan's influence has permeated Political Departments

The IRS scandal: Lois Lerner became director of the Exempt Organizations Unit of the Internal Revenue Service in 2005. She and her department were accused of singling out conservative and tea party groups for extra scrutiny when they applied for tax-exempt status. (6) Many had their applications delayed for months, and some for years. Despite the fact the actions of Mrs. Lerner and members of the Exempt Organization were illegal, they got off easy. (7)

The GSA Scandal: The General Services Administration, which oversees the managing of government buildings and real estate, provides product and service procurement support, and develops policies and relegations for the government, spent $822,000 of taxpayer money to fly 300 of its employees to a luxurious spa and casino outside Las Vegas for a conference in October of 2010. Its leaders had a goal to make their conference "over the top". The scandal forced the resignation of GSA chief, Martha Johnson, two of her top deputies and several other senior executives. (8) It brought to light the hundreds of millions of dollars the government spends on travel and conferences every year.

The Benghazi Scandal: The terrorist attack on the U.S. mission in Benghazi, Libya resulted in the death of Ambassador Christopher Stevens and three other Americans, Information Officer Sean Smith and two CIA operatives, Glen Doherty and Tyrone Woods, both former Navy Seals. (9) The Obama Admiration blamed the attack on a video that offended Muslims. An investigation by the House Select Committee provided evidence this was untrue. Many unanswered questions remain about the Benghazi Scandal. (10) Questions like, "Why was our Ambassador still in Benghazi when all other nations' ambassadors had been removed due to potential hostile threats?" "Why did our government not send forces to aid Christopher Stevens and others who were under attack for more than four hours?" "Why was it necessary for the Secretary of State, Hillary Clinton, to tell foreign dignitaries, a different account of what occurred in Benghazi than the account she presented to the families of those who died in Benghazi and the American people?" Many new and damning facts are surfacing concerning the deception and violations that occurred concerning what actually occurred at Benghazi.

The Obamacare Scandal: President Obama told the American people, "If you like your health plan, you can keep it. If you like your Doctors, you can keep them". (11) Both statements were false. Jonathan Gruber, a professor at MIT, an architect of Obamacare, said on National Television, "Lack of transparency is a huge political advantage...Basically, call it the stupidity of the American voter or whatever, but basically that was really critical to getting the thing to pass." (12)

For the first time in American history, Obamacare forced all Americans to purchase a product they may not want or face a fine from the Internal Revenue Service.

The Clinton Emails Scandal: Hillary Clinton, while serving as President Obama's Secretary of State, sent and received emails containing classified information through her unsecured email account. James Comey, the FBI Director, stated at a Congressional hearing, "Although there is evidence of potential violations of the statutes regarding the handling of classified information, our judgment is that no reasonable prosecutor would bring such a case. I know there will be intense public debate in the wake of this recommendation, as there was throughout this investigation." Evidence obtained indicates there would be no charges brought against Hillary

Clinton before the F.B.I interviewed her about what she did. The fact the F.B.I. did not placed Mrs. Clinton under oath before she was interviewed has caused many Americans to believe there was collusion between the leadership of the FBI and the Obama Administration concerning Hillary's actions. (13)

Director Comey shared with the Senate Committee, "There was evidence of potential violations of the statutes regarding Hillary's handling of classified information, but our judgment is that no reasonable prosecutor would bring such a case." Of whom was he referring to when he used the pronoun "Our"? Was he speaking specifically about members of the FBI? If that were the case, he was in error. The FBI does not have the authority to decide who should, or should not, be prosecuted for a crime. When the FBI finishes an investigation, it can, and usually does, make recommendations based on the evidence they have obtained. The information and evidence gathered in the course of an investigation is presented to the appropriate U.S. Attorney Department of Justice official, who will then determine whether prosecution or further action is warranted.

Some have suggested Director Comey's relationship to the Clintons caused him to treat Mrs. Clinton as he did. (14) During President Clinton's first term as president, questions began to surface concerning Bill and Hillary's involvement in the McDougal's law firm. A federal investigation, led by Robert Fish, discovered Bill Clinton pressured David Hale, a banker, to make an illegal federal-backed loan of $300,000 to Susan McDougal that would benefit both the Clinton's and the McDougal's. In the mid-1990's, James Comey joined the Senate Whitewater Committee that investigated the Clintons. There were no charges brought against the Clintons. The scandal concerning this issue eventually led to Independent

Counsel Kenneth Starr's discovery of Bill Clinton's involvement with Monica Lewinsky.

This same James Comey brought charges against Martha Stewart for conspiracy and obstruction of justice because she lied one time to the FBI. She received a prison sentence of five months. Yet, despite the fact Mrs. Clinton lied to the FBI, and to Congress, on numerous occasions, Director Comey did not suggest Mrs. Clinton be charged with obstruction of justice. (15)

Loretta Lynch should have made the decision to prosecute Hillary Clinton. She chose not to do so. Her ties to the Clintons could very well have influenced her decision not to file charges against Hillary. In 1999, President Bill Clinton nominated her to serve as the U.S. Attorney for the Eastern District of New York. She served in this capacity from 1991 to 2001. Hillary Clinton was elected to the United States Senate, representing New York, on January 3, 2001. In 2010, President Obama appointed Lynch to another term as U.S. Attorney for the Eastern District of New York. Hillary Clinton served as Secretary of State from 2009 to 2013. Was Lynch's appointment to be the U.S. Attorney for the Eastern District of New York twice during a time when Hillary was seeking political office coincidental?

President Obama nominated Lynch to become the Attorney General of the United States. She was confirmed on April 23, 2015 by a vote of 56 to 43. On June 27, 2016, Loretta Lynch and former President Bill Clinton met privately aboard Lynch's Justice Department jet, parked on the tarmac in Phoenix, Arizona. This meeting occurred while the FBI was investigating Mrs. Clinton for her misuse of top-secret information on her unsecured emails. When asked what they discussed in this meeting, she said, "The conversation involved personal social topics such as travels, golf and grandchildren." To her critics, concerning this meeting, she acknowledged how the meeting could raise questions and she would never do it again. She also stated she would accept the recommendation of the FBI on whether or not to prosecute Mrs. Clinton. Evidence recently uncovered, proves she had determined there would be no charges brought against Hillary Clinton. On June 8, 2017, Director Comey testified, under oath, that Loretta Lynch instructed him not to refer to the Clinton email scandal as an "investigation" but rather as a "matter." In June of 2017, the Senate Judiciary Committee began an investigation concerning Lynch's involvement in Hillary's email investigation.

Fast and Furious Scandal: Fast and Furious was a Bureau of Alcohol, Tobacco, Firearms, and Explosives operation in which the federal government allowed criminals to buy guns in Phoenix, Arizona area gun shops, with the intention of tracking them as they were transported into Mexico. The agency lost track of more than 1,400 of the 2,000 guns they allowed smugglers to buy. Two of these guns were located in an area where Mexicans, targeting illegal immigrants, killed Brian Terry, a Boarder Agent. Five years later, Brian Terry's family was still waiting for information about this incident from the Obama Administration. The House Oversight Committee released a scathing, report that found Holder's Justice Department held the facts from the loved ones of slain Border Patrol Agent, Brian Terry – seeing his family as more of a "nuisance" than ones deserving straight answers. This committee condemned Obama's assertion of executive privilege to deny Congress access to records pertaining to "Fast and Furious".

The Solyndra Scandal: Solyndra was a solar-panel company located in Silicon Valley, California. The company planned to build solar panels without polysilicon. While Solyndra's panels were more expensive to make, they advertised they were cheaper to install, and the skyrocketing price of polysilicon gave the company a chance to compete in the market. The Solyndra controversy was elevated to a scandal when the Office of Management and Budget officials in the Obama Administration felt pressured to approve a loan of $535 million despite an awareness of Solyndra's financial instability. When the Chinese firms began to overtake the solar-panel industry, the price of polysilicon began to fall sharply. As Solyndra's business began to fail, its financial officers made questionable financial decisions, which led to Solyndra shutting down, leaving 1,100 people out of work and taxpayers obligated for $535 million in federal loans.

The Selling of Uranium to Russia Scandal: The FBI discovered as early as 2009 evidence of bribery and corruption surrounding the controversial 2010 nuclear deal between the Obama Administration and Russia. (16) At issue is the 2010 sale of a Canadian company called Uranium One, which had extensive holdings in the United States, to a Russian entity. The deal allowed a subsidiary of Russia's government to gain control of 20 percent of U.S. uranium. The mining company, Uranium One, was originally based in South Africa, but merged in 2007 with Canada-based UrAsia Energy. Shareholders retained a controlling interest until 2010, when Russia's nuclear agency, completed purchase of a 51% stake. Hillary Clinton, as Secretary of State, played a part in the transaction because it involved the transfer of ownership of a material deemed important to national security. As the acquisition was taking place, the Clinton Foundation accepted contributions from nine individuals associated with Uranium One totaling more than $100 million.

Satan uses the Media to advance his Agenda

It is obvious, from a conservative point of view; many in the media in America today have a liberal bias. The views presented on NBC, CBS, MSNBC, CNN, The New York Times, and other liberal news outlets, concerning Donald Trump becoming president, presented a clear picture of bias before his election. (17) They openly laughed at the idea he would be the Republican candidate. After Donald Trump became the Republican candidate there was a constant barrage of negative comments made about him and anyone who supported him. The night of his election, television reporters stated that the election of Donald Trump was a colossal mistake for America and for the world. No president has come under such scrutiny by the media, as has Donald Trump. Ninety-two percent of the liberal news coverage concerning President Trump has been negative.

The news media clearly illustrates their favorable bias for Democrats and their social agenda. (18)The support for the Democratic candidate for President, Hillary Clinton, illustrates this fact. Despite the fact, many believe there is more than sufficient evidence against Mrs. Clinton to warrant her arrest on numerous charges; however, the liberal News Media has been very careful reporting anything negative against her. She misused top-secret emails on her unsecured, private server while serving as Secretary of State. FBI Director James Comey attested to this fact before Congress. He also shared the FBI had evidence to prove she destroyed evidence on her computer by using a software tool called BleachBit. Concerning her testimony before Congress, she denied there were top-secret emails on her computer. The news media shared, "She did not intend to deceive, and therefore she did not lie." She lied when she publicly blamed Bengasi on a video that dishonored Islam. While she was telling her daughter and Heads of State of other countries the truth, she was telling the families of those murdered in Bengasi, and the American people, a lie. She sold 20% of America's Uranium to the Russians, which was a violation of the law. (19) She was untruthful in her remarks about her part in buying the Russian Dossier to prove President Trump colluded with Russia in order to rig the presidential election. This Dossier contains numerous untrue statements. (20) She and the Democratic National Convention used dirty tricks against Bernie Sanders to secure the nomination, for her to become the Democrat Candidate for president. While there is plenty of evidence that Mrs. Clinton and the DNC colluded with the Russians, Robert Muller and his Grand Jury have found no evidence of collusion against President Trump with the Russians.

Satan uses protest

After police officer Darren Wilson shot Michael Brown, in Ferguson, Missouri in 2014, a witness said the police officer shot Brown while Brown was saying, "My hands are up, don't shoot." Despite the fact other witnesses said this was untrue, CNN and other news outlets continued to promote this narrative as a fact. On March 4, 2015, the U.S. Department of Justice reported at the conclusion of their investigation on this matter, "Forensic evidence supported the officer's account of the shooting."(21)The group, Black Lives Matter, some athletes, and several feminist groups, began to use the phrase "Hands up, don't shoot" or "Hands up" to protest against what they believed about police injustices against blacks.

Black Lives Matter groups, while protesting against the police shouted, "Pigs in a blanket fry them like bacon." They have blocked major highways, shutting down traffic for hours. Despite their protest marches and incendiary, hateful, and racist rhetoric against the police, the liberal news media have consistently elevated Black Lives Matter spokespersons without denouncing their radical views. (22) President Obama invited their leaders, DeRay Mckesson and Brittany Packnett, to the White House. (23) He said of these Black Life Matters leaders, "They are much better organizers than I was when I was their age, and I am confident that they are going to take America to new heights." His comments caused many to question President Obama's support for this organization. One can only imagine what would have been the results if a Republican president had invited the Grand Wizard of the KKK to the White House and made similar comments.

The current action by the National Football League's players to take a knee during the National Anthem has created division among many Americans. (24) Owners, and NFL leadership, have established rules in the past that prevented players from expressing their views on various issues. NFL Commissioner Roger Goodell threatened NFL players with fines who wanted to honor both 911 victims and the 5 police officers murdered in Dallas. Now, he says the NFL players have a first amendment right to protest. If it was inappropriate for Tim Tebow to offend fans who disagreed with his religious beliefs, to take a knee and pray, why is it acceptable for Colin Kaepernick and others to take a knee and offend fans who disagree with their politics?

Satan uses Religious scandals

Satan is very successful in attacking Christians and religious organizations. Political correctness has invaded the church, leaving many religious leaders and laypersons afraid to speak out against sin. Many preachers are fearful to preach against homosexuality for fear the IRS will revoke their church's 501 (c) 3 federal exempt status, or anger members of their church. There was an article in the Washington Post in August 2002 that reported a survey of 1,200 priest in which more than half stated there was a homosexual subculture in their diocese or seminary. (25) It is important to know and oppose the homosexual agenda. The Gay Rights Platform, constituted in Chicago in 1972, stated a desire to repeal all laws governing the age of sexual consent and to repeal all legislative provisions that restrict the sex or number of persons entering into a marriage union. They demanded anti-homophobic curriculum in the schools stressing the government should ensure all public education programs be designed to combat lesbian/gay prejudice. They demanded institutions that discriminate against lesbians and gay people be denied tax-exempt status and federal funding.

The homosexual agenda is an attempt to destroy Christianity, the concept of Scriptural marriage and the removal of all biblical principles that govern the Christian family. (26) Neither the Bible nor thousands of years of social practice agrees with the idea of same sex marriages. What the world condones today, the church will embrace within five years. Denominations such as The United Church of Christ, The Presbyterian Church (USA), and The Evangelical Lutheran Church of America have already sanctioned same sex marriages. Individual churches within other Demonization's have likewise sanctioned same sex marriages.

The purpose for Satan's attacks against religious leaders seems to be, "The larger the minister, the greater the publicity." Consider the following ministers that have fallen from prominence.

Ted Haggard: In 2006, Rev. Ted Haggard was removed as pastor of the New Life Church in Colorado Springs, for having a homosexual affair with a member of his church. New Life Church is a non-denominational, charismatic, Evangelical, megachurch that has more than 10,000 members. (27)

Jim Baker: Rev. Jim Baker was convicted in 1989 on Federal charges for misusing money designated for his ministry and sentenced to 45 years. His sentence was reduced to 8 years, with 5 years to serve. He was released from prison in 1994, is back in the ministry, and back on television. (28)

John Geoghan: John Geoghan was a Roman Catholic priest who served in Boston, Massachusetts. He was convicted as a serial child rapist in 2002. While serving time in maximum-security in Lancaster, Massachusetts, he was strangled and stomped to death in his cell by a fellow-inmate, Joseph Druce. (29)

Rabbi Fred Neulander: Rabbi Fred Neulander was a Reform rabbi in Cherry Hill, New Jersey who was convicted of hiring two men to murder his wife in 1994. He was sentenced to 30 years to life. (30)

Paul R. Shanley: Paul Shanley was a Catholic priest who served at St. Jean's Parish in Newton, Massachusetts. He was a prominent figure in the Boston clergy sex scandal. Shanley was convicted in 2002 of repeatedly raping boys over a period of years and served 12 years for child rape and was released in 2017. (31)

Sheikh Omar Abdel-Rahman: Sheikh Omar Abdel-Rahman was a blind Egyptian Muslim leader sentenced to a life sentence plus fifteen years, for his involvement in the bombing of the World Trade Center in 1993. Commonly known as "The Blind Sheikh," he hated Americans and Jews. He often called for the destruction of America and Israel. He died of natural causes on February 18, 2017 in the Federal Medical Center, Butner, in Bahama, North Carolina. (32)

Jimmy Swaggart: Rev. Jimmy Swaggart is a Pentecostal preacher and a televangelist. He often spoke out against preachers who had committed adultery in his messages, both at his church and in his Crusades. Pictures of Rev. Swaggart and a New Orleans prostitute, going in and out of a Motel, were sent to the Assemblies of God Denominational Headquarters. In 1988, Rev. Swaggart admitted to his sin and tearfully apologized.(33)

Satan uses the Confederate flag and statues

For more than one hundred years, Confederate flags (34), and statutes (35), have dotted the Southern landscape. Now, these flags and statutes are offensive. If they are offensive now, why were they not offensive during the Kennedy Administration when the African-American Freedom Riders of 1961 traveled along segregated bus routes in the South? Why was there no outcry to have them removed then? Some believe the Confederate flag and statues represent segregation and are a constant reminder of the days of slavery by Southerners. If this is a true representation of this flag and these statues how do, those who hold this view explain the fact there were slaves in all of the old colonies and there is no outcry against the Union flag? Philadelphia, Rhode Island, Boston, and New York auctioned slaves. If this flag and these statues are offensive, why was there no outcry against them when The Civil Rights Act of 1964, which outlawed discrimination based on race, color, religion, sex, or national origin, was established? Why now? Some would have us believe this is a backlash from the shooting in June of 2015, when Dylann Roof, a white supremacist, shot and killed nine African Americans in a prayer service at Emanuel African Methodist Episcopal Church in Charleston, South Carolina. Others believe this is part of the Democrat agenda to support their African American base. Nancy Pelosi, a Democratic Congresswoman from California, and the House Minority Leader, said on national television, "If Republicans are serious about rejecting white supremacy, I call upon Speaker Ryan to join Democrats to remove the Confederate statues from the Capitol immediately."(36) More Republicans voted for the

Civil Rights Act than Democrats did. Why now? Is this just another part of Satan's plan to divide America?

Satan masquerades as an Angel of light

Satan is the source of evil in this world. Satan is behind the deaths caused by abortion and sexually transmitted disease. He rules in the hearts of the world's dictators, who cause their people misery, hardship, and death. He influences politicians, who favor power over being servants for the good of those who elected them. He shrouds God's truth and distorts the hearts of homosexuals, enabling them to believe a lie (Romans 1:28). He fills the heart of preachers with fear, preventing them from preaching God's word, thus causing nations to turn away from God's truths and embrace Satan's lies (Lamentations 4:13). Jesus describes Satan as "The thief (who) cometh not, but for to steal, and to kill, and to destroy...." (John 10:10). In John 8:44, Jesus says of Satan, "...He was a murderer from the beginning, and abode not in the truth, because there is no truth in him. When he speaketh a lie, he speaketh of his own: for he is a liar, and the father of it." In that, God alone can overpower Satan. We need to pray for deliverance from Satan's power and influence in our lives and in our world.

We need to look at what is going on behind the scenes and carefully examine the corruption that is taking place in this world. The church and Christians are under attack today as never before. John says that Satan is the accuser of the brethren before God day and night (Revelations 12:10). As mortals, we do not have the power or the ability to combat Satan on our own. We need protection from Satan's power. We need God! David says, "For the LORD God is a sun and shield: the LORD will give grace and glory: no good thing will he withhold from them that walk uprightly: (Psalm 84:11). When we pray, we need to ask God to help us take "...the shield of faith, wherewith (we) shall be able to quench all the fire darts of the wicked (one)" (Ephesians 6:16).

Deception has become an epidemic in America. We often forget Satan has come to masquerade as an angel of light. He distorts the truth, uses lies, good intentions, and good and decent people, to achieve his objectives. Satan is successful as a deceiver to create doubt, to divide and to destroy America. Americans are divided over politicians, religious leaders, the effectiveness of governmental departments, and the ability of the news media to be truthful. Satan's deception has many Americans asking, "Who can I believe?" or "What is the truth?"

In a Televised speech in 1960, Nikita Khrushchev, the General Secretary of the Communist Party and leader of the U.S.S.R, said of America:

> Your children's children will live under communism. You Americans are so gullible. No, you won't accept Communism outright; but we'll keep feeding you small doses of Socialism until you will finally wake up and find that you already have Communism. We won't have to fight you; We'll so weaken your economy, until you fall like overripe fruit into our hands. (37)

In the midst of all the doubt and division-taking place, American's faith in God, and the truth of His Word, is negatively impacted. Spiritually, America is in decline. Most Christian denominations are reporting declines in membership, weekly attendance, baptisms, and financial giving. Despite this fact, many Americans believe America remains a Christian nation, while large numbers of young adults and youth have turned their back on the church. To increase membership and provide more money to sustain a church, churches are becoming entertainment centers. America is a nation in transition and in the process of forsaking her religious roots. Most politicians are more concerned about power, prestige, and money than what is Godly, morally or socially good for the American people. Most ministers are more concerned in appeasing their congregation than they are in pleasing God.

Attacks against Christianity

At the Senate Judiciary Committee hearing for Amy Coney Barrett, a law professor at the Notre Dame University, and President Trump's nominee to the Seventh Circuit Court of Appeals, was questioning, suggested that Barrett's Catholic faith might disqualify her from serving as a judge. During a contentious confirmation hearing for Russell Vought, President Trump's nominee for Deputy Director of the Office of Management and Budget, Bernie Sanders, a Vermont senator, questioned Vought's faith, implying Vought was Islamophobic. (38) The actions of these senators call into question their anti-Christian bias.

Satan's attacks against Christianity are dividing America. A teacher in New Jersey, Walter Tutka, was suspended for giving a Bible to a student. (39) Coach Joe Kennedy in Washington was placed on leave for saying a prayer with his players on the field after a football game. (40) The Fire Chief in Atlanta, Kelvin Cochran, was fired for publishing a book that defended Christianity against immoral social issues. (41) A Marine, Lance Corporal Monifa Sterling, was court-martialed for refusing to remove a Bible verse from her desk. (42) Christians are referred to as "bigots" and "racists." Christianity has become a punching bag for stand-up comedians. Assembly Bill 2943 is a proposed California bill that, if passed, would censor biblical preaching, teaching, and religious material. (43) If this bill passes, individuals will be fined for preaching or teaching biblical truths that might offend those who support the homosexual agenda. It would also restrict individuals from purchasing books or hearing someone preach or teach anything considered offensive to the homosexual agenda.

At a march at Stanford University on Jan 19, 1988, five hundred students marched shouting, "Hey, hey, ho, ho, Western Culture's got to go." (44) What does "Western Culture" mean? This term refers to the Judeo Christian civilization to describe the social norms, ethical values, traditional customs, belief systems, and political systems that govern America's society.

The past twenty-five to thirty years has brought about a radical change to the culture of America. There is no place in America that demonstrates the attack on Western Culture more so than in our schools. Liberalism has permeated our colleges and Universities. The teachers our colleges and universities are producing demonstrate this fact. American heritage, Judeo-Christianity, Gun rights and the Constitution are all under attack through the curriculum of our schools. The educational system of America is promoting Socialism, sexual freedom, government dependency, and Islam. Is it any wonder that 58% of Millennials favor Socialism?

The very fiber of Christianity is under attack. Church members seldom hear doctrinal messages on judgment and Christian accountability. The silence from pulpits on the subject of hell gives evidence many pastors no longer believe in the reality of hell, or they are afraid to preach on the subject for fear of offending members of their congregation.

American's attire has changed. Wearing your pants down around your knees has become the style for many youth of this generation. It is both obscene and offensive. The attire at churches has changed. Casual has become the norm. However, the Casual attire in churches fits well with the commitment of many church members. The use of vulgarity no longer offends many today. The use of drugs is replacing smoking cigarettes, cigars, and pipes. Movies no longer just tell a story, they seek to indoctrinate a perverted lifestyle.

As America's demographics have changed so has its culture. In days past, when those from other countries came to America, they sought to embrace Americanism. They learned the language and embraced the Western Culture. This is no longer the case. Today, many of those who come from other countries to America isolate themselves from Americans, demanding the rights and privileges of America while refusing to assimilate into the American society. There is no other culture in the world that grants the privileges that the Western Culture of America grants to its citizens. However, some hold the view, the Western Culture favors one race over another; therefore, this view must be changed.

Is America on the verge of revival?

Despite America's spiritual depravity, many preachers tell their congregations, "America is on the verge of a great revival." Is America on the verge of Revival? The answer to this question depends on where we are concerning the coming of Christ. If we are on the verge of the Coming of Christ, we are not on the verge of a national revival. The Bible clearly teaches these two events cannot and will not occur simultaneously. The New Testament teaches, prior to the coming of Christ, times will digress to a time of deception (Matthew 24:5), to a time of division (Luke 12:53), and to a time of destruction (John 16:2). Paul tells us in II Timothy 2:3, "Let no man deceive you by any means: for that day shall not come, except there come a falling away first, and that man of sin be revealed, the son of perdition." The spiritual depravity of America and the church indicates the "falling away" is already occurring.

The Bible clearly reveals the following events that will occur prior to the coming of Christ.

1. Jeremiah 31:1-3 - tells us Israel will become a Nation again. This event occurred on May 14, 1948.
2. Matthew 24:32-34 - reveals that when Israel is restored as a Nation, Christ will return in that generation.
3. Revelation 3:14-22 - reveals, just before Christ returns, the church will be so spiritually depraved it will not be able to recognize its own spiritual depravity.
4. Matthew 24:6 - tells us there will be wars and rumors of wars. In 2013, the U.S. Special Operations Command (SOCOM) stated they had special operations forces in 134 countries, where they were either involved in combat, special missions or advising and training foreign forces.
5. John 16:2 - tells us there will be persecution of Christians. More than one hundred million Christians are undergoing persecution in the world today. The Center for the Study of Global Christianity, an academic research center that monitors worldwide demographic trends in Christianity, estimates between the years 2005 and 2015, that 900,000 Christians were martyred, an average of 90,000 Christians each year.
6. Luke 21:11 - tells us there will be pestilence - contagious diseases. Millions around the world die each year from diseases.
    a. Malaria - Over one million people die from malaria each year, mostly children under five years of age, with ninety percent of malaria cases occurring in Sub-Saharan Africa. An estimated 300-600 million people suffer from malaria each

year. More than forty percent of the world's population lives in malaria-risk areas.
b. Tuberculosis - Tuberculosis is one of the world's deadliest diseases: One third of the world's population is infected with Tuberculosis. In 2015, 10.4 million people around the world became sick with this disease.
c. Measles - is a highly contagious infection caused by the measles virus. In 2012, 122,000 people, mostly children, died from measles worldwide.
d. Famine - BBC News reported that a child dies in the world every ten seconds from starvation. A report from The United Nations Food and Agriculture Organization estimates, between the years of 2014 to 2016, approximately 795 million people in the world were suffering from chronic malnutrition.
e. Earthquakes will increase. The National Earthquake Information Center now locates about 20,000 earthquakes each year, or approximately 55 per day.
f. Israel will be the focal point of concern just prior to the Second Coming of Christ Zechariah 12:2-3 says, "Jerusalem will become a cup of trembling and a burdensome stone for all people" prior to the coming of Christ. Consider what is taking place in Israel today.

We do not know the time of His coming, but we are living in the times of His coming. In 2017, attendees of the Southern Baptist Convention in Phoenix, Arizona were informed weekly worship attendance in their churches declined by 97,000 from 2014 to 2015. Some would say this is just a phase; this will improve. Yet, the Southern Baptist

Convention has lost membership for the past ten consecutive years. The decline in membership and weekly attendance is also true for most churches in other denominations, as well. Jesus shared, in Revelation 2:1-7, the church at Ephesus, had lost their first love, and if they did not repent, they would be prevented from shining the light of the gospel into their city. Is this why the light of the gospel has grown dim through the church of today? Evangelism in most churches has become a burden, and lost souls are no longer a priority.

The church has been given a responsibility that Christ takes very seriously, as mentioned in Ezekiel 3:16-19:

> At the end of seven days the word of the Lord came to me, saying, "Son of man, I have appointed you a watchman to the house of Israel; whenever you hear a word from My mouth, warn them from Me. When I say to the wicked, "you will surely die; and you do not warn him or speak out to warn the wicked from his wicked way that he may live, that wicked man shall die in his iniquity, but his blood I will require at your hand. Yet if you have warned the wicked and he does not turn from his wickedness or from his wicked way, he shall die in his iniquity: but you have delivered yourself.

The condition of the church indicates many, who profess Christ as their Savior, do not take their spiritual responsibility seriously. Matthew tells us in Matthew 24:12, "...because wickedness shall abound, the love of many shall wax cold." Based on the lifestyle of many in the church, most church members today are either lost or carnal. The saved and spirit-filled members, in the church have decreased to the point many churches no longer are able to maintain a sustainable and effective ministry. The lost members have no concern for advancing the kingdom of God. The carnal members of churches are injurious, both to the lost and to the saved. The un-Christian lifestyle of the carnal Christian gives support to the lost, causing the lost to believe they are spiritually sound. The absence of commitment of carnal church members is injurious to the cause of Christ because they refuse to assist committed Christians in advancing the kingdom of God. The failure of both the lost and carnal members reveal many church members doubt the power of God, distrust the love of God, and disbelieve the Word of God.

Deuteronomy 28 records a long list of remedial judgments God will place on a nation that does not obey His Word. These judgments include such things as natural disasters, political confusion and corruption, crop failures, economic calamities, rebellious youth, rampant disease, epidemics of divorce, defeat in war, including giving the nation the kind of leaders it deserves. This sounds like a description of America.

If the people of a nation refuse to repent, God will deliver that nation to destruction. Many years after Jonah, God sent another prophet to Nineveh, a prophet by the name of Nahum. This time, Nahum was told that Nineveh had (notice these words) "an incurable wound" (Nahum 3:19). This time, there was no repentance among the Ninevites. When the wound becomes incurable, God will destroy a nation.

What relevance does the second coming of Christ have on God's judgment on America?

Often, when I preach in Evangelism Conferences, I ask the question, "How many of you believe we are on the verge of a great revival?" There is a loud shout of "Amen." I then ask, "How many of you believe we are on the verge of the coming of Christ?" Again, there is a loud shout of "Amen." I then share, "It cannot be both. The Bible teaches that prior to the coming of Christ, conditions within the church and the world will grow worse. Everywhere I look, I see evidence the church and the world are growing spiritually worse. I believe we are on the verge of the coming of Christ, but not on the verge of a national revival."

The Jews are God's chosen people, therefore, to know what God is doing, watch the Nation of Israel. Zachariah 14:1-2, reveals, just prior to the coming of Christ, Jerusalem will undergo a time of devastation.

> Behold, the day of the LORD cometh, and thy spoil shall be divided in the midst of thee. For I will gather all nations against Jerusalem to battle; and the city shall be taken, and the houses rifled, and the women ravished; and half of the city shall go forth into captivity, and the residue of the people shall not be cut off from the city.

Israel's enemies are divided into two groups: the surrounding Islamic nations that have historically been their enemies in past wars and radical terrorist organizations, formed more recently, who are committed to Israel's destruction. The hatred for Israel by her neighbors is a common theme on daily news programs. Currently, thirty-one United Nations Member States refuse to recognize Israel as a state. The Palestinians, Syrians, Jordanians, Turks, and Iranians all boast of their intent to rid the world of a Jewish nation. The PLO, Hamas, Fatah, Hezbollah, and Isis have been created to commit terror attacks against Israel and her allies. It is of interest to note these organizations were birthed in the last sixty years. The Bible teaches that in the generation of the rebirth of Israel, Christ will return (Matthew 24:34).

Zachariah 12:3 reveals, prior to the coming of Christ, all nations will gather against Israel. The question I have often asked myself is, "In that Israel is one of America's greatest allies; if Israel is attacked militarily, what would prevent America from coming to Israel's aid?" The only answer I can conceive is, "America will be unable to respond to Israel's defense." How is this possible when, at this current time, America has the strongest military in the world? I believe the answer is God's judgment against America will render America unable to provide Israel with military assistance.

The New Testament reveals that in the last days, the world and the church will undergo difficult times. Yet, despite the clear and present danger the Bible outlines for the world and the church during the last days, many church leaders are choosing to ignore these truths and proclaim a message that declares, "We are on the verge of the coming of Christ, and at the same time, on the verge of a great revival."

If we are on the verge of the coming of Christ, America and the world are not on the verge of revival. I understand this is not a popular view. I also understand Paul's admonition to Timothy in II Timothy 4:3-4:

> For the time will come when they will not endure sound doctrine; but after their own lusts shall they heap to themselves teachers, having itching ears. And they shall turn away their ears from the truth, and shall be turned unto fables.

When God called Jeremiah to share His message with Judah, Jeremiah faced a spiritually depraved nation that viewed themselves as righteous and resented God's message, which accused them of their sinfulness. Judah had become so sinful, God declared them incurable (II Chronicles 36:16). They became angry at Jeremiah's messages that accused them of sin. They criticized him, beat him, imprisoned him, and tried to kill him. Despite the fact, Jeremiah confronted them with God's truth; they refused to believe his messages were from God. Jeremiah's time parallels America today. America is sinful; however, most Americans do not believe they are sinful to the point of deserving God's judgment. The message of most preachers is peace, protection, and prosperity. I believe God has declared America incurable and His judgment upon America is imminent.

The spiritual condition of America is a reflection of the spiritual condition of the church. Jeremiah said his nation failed because of the sins of the preachers of his day (Lamentations 4:13). Today, as church members become less spiritual, messages from pulpits illustrate a fearful reluctance to condemn a sinful lifestyle. The desire to reach people has shifted from a spiritual perspective to that of a desire for numbers and cash. Easy believism has become the norm. What most profess to believe makes little or no difference in the way they live. The church and the world are suffering from an absence of biblical truth.

In an attempt to attract younger members, churches have become a smorgasbord of worship styles, seeking to reach the masses. If there has ever been a time when our world needs to hear the whole truth of God's Word, it is today! Doctoral and expository preaching has been replaced with topical messages emphasizing the love of God. Most American's no longer believe God judge's sin or that hell is real. The message from pulpits has led many to believe, "You can believe what you want, live as you please, and when you die you will go to heaven." As convinced as one may be this opinion is truth; it is not. The message of the Bible is very clear about the path and purpose of salvation. If we are on the verge of Christ's Second Coming, neither America nor the world is on the verge of revival.

Will America undergo judgment before The Second Coming?

God is the rightful arbiter of judgment. God is depicted as the Judge of the world in Genesis 18:25 when Abraham pleaded with God concerning His judgment on Sodom, by saying, "...shall not the judge of all the earth do right?" The Psalmist, in Psalms 75:7, tells us, "...God is the judge: that putteth down one, and setteth up another." Matthew tells us in Matthew 25:32-33, "And before him shall be gathered all nations: and he shall separate them one from another as a shepherd divideth his sheep from the goats: and he set the sheep on his right hand, but the goats on the left." Despite the fact the people of Judah were very knowledgeable of God's judgment against sinful nations, they refused to believe God would judge them. Having said this, permit me to ask you a question, "If God judged Judah, for the same sins America is guilty of; will He not also judge America?"

The idea that America will collapse seems an impossibility to most Americans. The People of Judah had the same belief about Jerusalem. Jeremiah said of Jerusalem, in Lamentations 4:12, "The kings of the earth, and all the inhabitants of the world, would not have believed that the adversary and the enemy should have entered into the gates of Jerusalem." The people of Judah believed they were God's chosen people. It would appear they believed God was obligated to bless them no matter how they lived. American's are of the same mindset. The moral and spiritual depravity occurring in America today is the reason America is in the same condition Judah was in during the days of Jeremiah--beyond redemption.

Chapter 2

GOD JUDGED JUDAH

Why is it important to examine God's judgment of Judah during the days of Jeremiah? Does God's judgment of Judah during this period have any significance for America? As one walks through the book of Jeremiah, they will soon discover God's judgment of Judah was the result of Judah's leadership and the people of Judah failing to obey God, and their unwillingness to repent. The political leaders of America have long abandoned America's founding, Christian principles. America has failed God and no longer considers Him as Sovereign. America is as politically and spiritually corrupt today as Judah was during the days of Jeremiah. America's political leaders are not elected for their spiritual qualities, but rather for their social and economic promises. Elections occur with little regard for the present spiritual condition of our nation.

Most Americans have no idea what the Bible teaches about the antichrist and his rule over a one-world government. The current cry from politicians, for "open boarders" and "a global government" is satanic. The world's population is growing restless and clamoring for answers to its many problems. The depraved condition in which the world finds itself has many crying for a world leader. Satan will present the antichrist to solve the world's problems. He will provide solution to problems between Israel and her enemies. He will negotiate a peace agreement between Israel and her Arab neighbors only to break it after three and a half years. Most of the world's population, and most in the church, have no idea this coming world leader will be the Antichrist. Nor do they know the Antichrist's coming is to overthrow God and His redemptive plan for humanity. Neither do they know the church is Satan's primary instrument to prepare humanity for the acceptance of the Antichrist. Satan has so distorted God's Word that most have no concept of biblical truth.

The background for Jeremiah's ministry

The nation of Israel was divided after the death of Solomon. Ten of the twelve tribes remained in their current location and maintained the name of Israel. Two tribes, the tribes of Judah and Benjamin, and many of the tribe of Levi - the priestly tribe – claimed the Southern territory of the previous State of Israel and became the nation of Judah. As time progressed, God judged Israel and the Assyrians carrying them away into captivity. Over the next one hundred years, Judah's sinfulness progressed to the point God declared Judah incurable (II Chronicles 36:16). The sins for which God judged Judah are the same sins America is guilty of today. It is important to re-examine God's judgment of Judah because, if God would judge His chosen people for the same sins America is committing, is it not reasonable to believe, God will judge America?

Judah no longer believed God was sovereign

The book of Jeremiah brings us to a period when Judah no longer heeded God's warnings, shunned the sovereignty of God, and refused to believe God would judge their disobedience. Through Jeremiah, God shared His messages against Judah for their sinfulness and His repeated call for the people of Judah to repent. Jeremiah describes Judah's cold and unapologetic remarks of denial of their sinfulness and their refusal to repent.

Judah had sunk to such a depraved spiritual state; God's judgment became imminent. What is said of the church at Laodicea, in Revelation 3:17, could be said of the people of Judah. "Because thou sayest, I am rich, and increased with goods, and have need of nothing; and knowest not that thou art wretched, and miserable, and poor, and blind, and naked." Judah became spiritually depraved. They were guilty of forsaking God, worshiped false gods, and consumed with a lust for self-interests. Corruption became prevalent in their government. They no longer were concerned about God's requirements for their leaders, (Deuteronomy 17:14-20). They dishonored God in their businesses and their daily dealings with others (Jeremiah 5:20-29)). Even the religious establishment was corrupt. Jeremiah tells us in Jeremiah 5:31, "The prophets prophesy falsely, and the priests bear rule by their means; and my people love to have it so: and what will ye do in the end thereof?" Their worship became corrupt; prostitution became a part of the worship services in several of their false religions (Jeremiah 13:27).

It was not that the people of Judah did not know God's requirements for them, they no longer cared (Jeremiah 2:19). They were willing to acknowledge God, but unwilling to give God His rightful place in their life (Jeremiah 2:31). To them, God had become just another god among the many other gods they chose to worship. Because of their disobedience, God would utter His "...judgments against them, touching all their wickedness, who have forsaken me, and have burned incense unto other gods, and worshipped the works of their own hands." (Jeremiah 1:16).

The leadership of Judah had forsaken God.

Scriptures reveal, while God sometimes decides who will be the leader of a nation, He also allows leaders whose values are not those taught in the Bible. In Exodus 9:16, God appointed Pharaoh King over Egypt. In Daniel 4:17, God appointed Nebuchadnezzar to be king over Babylon. Scriptures also record that nations have chosen leaders who were not God's choice. God said of Israel, "They have set up kings, but not by me: they have made princes, and I knew it not: of their silver and their gold have they made them idols, that they may be cut off" (Hosea 8:4). The Psalmist tells us when God is exalted as Lord over a nation, that nation is blessed (Psalms 33:12). When a nation's leaders do not recognize and submit to the sovereignty of God, that nation will come under God's judgment (Isaiah 60:12).

God's requirements for a King

God gave eight requirements for the Jewish people to be required of their king.

1. He must be chosen by God
2. He must be a Jew
3. He must place his faith in God for the protection and provision for his people
4. He must encourage his people to place their faith in God for their needs
5. He must not have many wives that would turn him away from God
6. He should not use his office to become rich
7. He should make the Word of God a priority in his life and through his decisions as the King

8. He should not place himself above those of whom he serves

Moses shared these requirements in Deuteronomy 17:14-20.

> When thou art come unto the land which the LORD thy God giveth thee, and shalt possess it, and shalt dwell therein, and shalt say, I will set a king over me, like as all the nations that are about me; Thou shalt in any wise set him king over thee, whom the LORD thy God shall choose: one from among thy brethren shalt thou set king over thee: thou mayest not set a stranger over thee, which is not thy brother. But he shall not multiply horses to himself, nor cause the people to return to Egypt, to the end that he should multiply horses: forasmuch as the LORD hath said unto you, Ye shall henceforth return no more that way. Neither shall he multiply wives to himself, that his heart turn not away: neither shall he greatly multiply to himself silver and gold. And it shall be, when he sitteth upon the throne of his kingdom, that he shall write him a copy of this law in a book out of that which is before the priests the Levites: And it shall be with him, and he shall read therein all the days of his life: that he may learn to fear the LORD his God, to keep all the words of this law and these statutes, to do them: That his heart be not lifted up above his brethren, and that he turn not aside from the commandment, to the right hand, or to the left: to the end that he may

prolong his days in his kingdom, he, and his children, in the midst of Israel.

To understand the ministry of Jeremiah and God's judgment against Judah, it is important to examine the leaders of Judah, who had a personal part in God's judgment upon Judah.

King Hezekiah

Hezekiah was a godly king who loved and served God. In Isaiah 37, Isaiah reveals when Sennacherib, king of the Assyrians, sent 185,000 troops to conquer Jerusalem, he mocked the power of God and the Jewish people. Sennacherib reminded Hezekiah and the people of Jerusalem how he, and his army, had defeated other nations. When Hezekiah received Sennacherib's threating letter, he went up to the House of the Lord and began to pray. God sent Hezekiah an answer to his pray through the prophet, Isaiah, informing him not to worry. God's word to Hezekiah was, "Sennacherib needs to remember who I am and what I have done." That night God sent an Angel who killed the 185,000 troops. When Sennacherib returned to Nineveh and was worshipping his god, Nisroch, he was murdered by two of his sons. There is no doubt this incident of God's divine protection for Jerusalem, associated with a prayer from the House of Lord, remained in the minds of the people of Judah.

Within a short period after the 185,000 Assyrian troops were destroyed, Hezekiah became critically ill (Isaiah 38). God informed him to write out his will and prepare to die. Hezekiah goes back to the House of the Lord and weeps before God, pleading with the Lord to extend his life. Once again, God sends His answer to Hezekiah's prayer through Isaiah. Isaiah informed Hezekiah that God had heard his prayer and would extend his life by an additional fifteen years. We know from comparing II Kings 18:2 with II Kings 20:6, Hezekiah was 39 years old when he received his message from God that he would soon die. After God spared his life and gave him an additional fifteen years to live, he did a very foolish thing.

God's destruction of the 185,000, made Hezekiah's fame spread throughout the territory. Sennacherib, the king of Babylon, heard Hezekiah had been sick and sent him letters expressing his sorrow for his sickness and presented him with a present in an attempt to make him feel better. Hezekiah was so impressed by the kindness shown to him by the king of Babylon, he gave the king's representatives a tour of Jerusalem, showing them everything, his wealth, his armament, his defense, his troop strength, etc. He foolishly provided ammunition to his nation's enemy. Isaiah rebuked Hezekiah for his foolishness. God pronounced judgment on Hezekiah's family and the nation of Judah to be executed at some future date after his death (II Kings 20: 17-18).

Note what Hezekiah did and why God punished his family and his nation for his foolishness.

> At that time Berodachbaladan, the son of Baladan, king of Babylon, sent letters and a present unto Hezekiah: for he had heard that Hezekiah had been sick. And Hezekiah hearkened unto them, and shewed them all the house of his precious things, the silver, and the gold, and the spices, and the precious ointment, and all the house of his armour, and all that was found in his treasures: there was nothing in his house, nor in all his dominion, that Hezekiah shewed them not. Then came Isaiah the prophet unto king Hezekiah, and said unto him,

> What said these men? and from whence came they unto thee? And Hezekiah said, They are come from a far country, even from Babylon. And he said, What have they seen in thine house? And Hezekiah answered, All the things that are in mine house have they seen: there is nothing among my treasures that I have not shewed them. And Isaiah said unto Hezekiah, Hear the word of the LORD. Behold, the days come, that all that is in thine house, and that which thy fathers have laid up in store unto this day, shall be carried into Babylon: nothing shall be left, saith the LORD. And of thy sons that shall issue from thee, which thou shalt beget, shall they take away; and they shall be eunuchs in the palace of the king of Babylon. Then said Hezekiah unto Isaiah, Good is the word of the LORD which thou hast spoken. And he said, Is it not good, if peace and truth be in my days? (2 Kings 20:12-19).

Hezekiah's remarks provides no evidence he was sorry for his actions. He was pleased when he heard the punishment for his actions would be implemented after his death (II Kings 20:19).

King Manasseh

When Hezekiah died, his son, Manasseh, became king. Manasseh was a son who was born during Hezekiah's extended fifteen-year life span. Manasseh was the worst king in the history of Judah. He was 12 years old when he became king and reigned 55 years (II Kings 21:1-2). Despite the fact

Manasseh's father loved God and Mannasseh had often heard of the supernatural miracles God had performed for his father and his nation, Manasseh refused to honor and worship God. II Kings 21:1-12 records the following about Manasseh:

> Manasseh was twelve years old when he began to reign, and reigned fifty and five years in Jerusalem. And his mother's name was Hephzibah. And he did that which was evil in the sight of the LORD, after the abominations of the heathen, whom the LORD cast out before the children of Israel. For he built up again the high places which Hezekiah his father had destroyed; and he reared up altars for Baal, and made a grove, as did Ahab king of Israel; and worshipped all the host of heaven, and served them. And he built altars in the house of the LORD, of which the LORD said, In Jerusalem would I put my name. And he built altars for all the host of heaven in the two courts of the house of the LORD. And he made his son pass through the fire, observed times, used enchantments, and dealt with familiar spirits and wizards: he wrought much wickedness in the sight of the LORD, to provoke him to anger. And he set a graven image of the grove that he had made in the house, of which the LORD said to David, and to Solomon his son, In this house, and in Jerusalem, which I have chosen out of all tribes of Israel, will I put my name for ever: Neither will I make the feet of Israel move any more out of the land which I gave their fathers; only if they will observe to

do according to all that I have commanded them, and according to all the law that my servant Moses commanded them. But they hearkened not: and Manasseh seduced them to do more evil than did the nations whom the LORD destroyed before the children of Israel. And the LORD spake by his servants the prophets, saying, Because Manasseh king of Judah hath done these abominations, and hath done wickedly above all that the Amorites did, which were before him, and hath made Judah also to sin with his idols: Therefore thus saith the LORD God of Israel, Behold, I am bringing such evil upon Jerusalem and Judah, that whosoever heareth of it, both his ears shall tingle. And I will stretch over Jerusalem the line of Samaria, and the plummet of the house of Ahab: and I will wipe Jerusalem as a man wipeth a dish, wiping it, and turning it upside down.

Manasseh's Conversion

The biblical description of Manasseh presents one so vile he caused the streets of Jerusalem to run with the blood of innocent people. Not only did he murder the innocent, he made them suffer. Many theologians believe he was the one who caused the death of Isaiah by having him sawed in half. He rejected everything his father promoted about God and worshipped numerous idols and false gods. Because of his sinfulness, God also declared judgment upon the nation of Judah (II Kings 24:3). Yet, when the Assyrians captured Manasseh, during his incarceration, he repented with great sorrow (II Chronicles 33:12). God forgave him and allowed him to escape and return as king of Judah. As a repentant sinner, he began to correct all the sinful things he had done. Despite his repentance God did not forget His promise to judge Judah because of Manasseh's sinfulness (II Kings 23:26) II Chronicles 33:9-16 records Manasseh's repentance and commitment to God.

> So Manasseh made Judah and the inhabitants of Jerusalem to err, and to do worse than the heathen, whom the LORD had destroyed before the children of Israel. And the LORD spake to Manasseh, and to his people: but they would not hearken. Wherefore the LORD brought upon them the captains of the host of the king of Assyria, which took Manasseh among the thorns, and bound him with fetters, and carried him to Babylon. And when he was in affliction, he besought the LORD his God, and humbled himself greatly before the God of his fathers, And prayed unto him: and he was intreated of him, and heard his supplication, and brought him again to Jerusalem into his kingdom. Then Manasseh knew that the LORD he was God. Now after this he built a wall without the city of David, on the west side of Gihon, in the valley, even to the entering in at the fish gate, and compassed about Ophel, and raised it up a very great height, and put captains of war in all the fenced cities of Judah. And he took away the strange gods, and the idol out of the house of the LORD, and all the altars that he had

built in the mount of the house of the LORD, and in Jerusalem, and cast them out of the city. And he repaired the altar of the LORD, and sacrificed thereon peace offerings and thank offerings, and commanded Judah to serve the LORD God of Israel.

King Amon

Amon was 22 years old when his father, Manasseh, died and he became king. He was as vile as his father had been. In fact, Amon was so vile his servants killed him after only two years as king. After Amon's servants murdered him, the people of Judah put each of Amon's servants to death that had a part in his death. The history of Amon's short reign as king is recorded in II Kings 21:19-24:

> Amon was twenty and two years old when he began to reign, and he reigned two years in Jerusalem. And his mother's name was Meshullemeth, the daughter of Haruz of Jotbah. And he did that which was evil in the sight of the LORD, as his father Manasseh did. And he walked in all the way that his father walked in, and served the idols that his father served, and worshipped them: And he forsook the LORD God of his fathers, and walked not in the way of the LORD. And the servants of Amon conspired against him, and slew the king in his own house. And the people of the land slew all them that had conspired against king Amon; and the people of the land made Josiah his son king in his stead.

King Josiah

After Amon's death, Josiah, Amon's son and Manasseh's grandson, became the king of Judah. Josiah's reign as king stands in sharp contrast to that of both his father and grandfather. The author of II Kings says of Josiah, "And like unto him was there no king before him, that turned to the Lord with all his heart, and with all his soul, and with all his might, according to all the law of Moses; neither after him arose there any like him" (II Kings 23:25).

The Bible does not tell us when Manasseh was captured by the Assyrians, how long he was imprisoned, how he escaped, nor how he regained his throne in Judah. We are only told that, during Manasseh's incarceration, he was genuinely converted and became a devoted follower of God (II Chronicles 33:12-13). When he returned to Babylon, he sought to correct the sinful mistakes he had made in the past (II Chronicles 33:14-20). Though Manasseh's conversion had no positive impact on his son Amon, his conversion appears to have had a positive impact upon his grandson Josiah.

Josiah became king at the age of eight and reigned for thirty-one years. At age 16, he began to seek the Lord and committed himself to God's will (II Chronicles 34:3-7). At age twenty, he began to cleanse his nation of sinful activity (II Chronicles 34:3

At age 20:

- He destroyed all the pagan shrines, the Asherah poles and images of other gods.
- He tore down the images of Baal.
- He abolished idol worship and had the places dedicated for idol worship destroyed and removed.
- He had the priest put to death who had forsaken God, and promoted and practiced idol worship.

- He destroyed the houses where homosexuals practiced their sinful acts near the House of the Lord.
- He stopped the practice of the Occult and Spiritism.
- He stopped the practice of child-sacrifice to the god Molech.
- He reinstated the Feast of Passover that had not been conducted since the days of Samuel (II Chronicles 35:18).

At age 26, he began a campaign to refurbish the House of the Lord (II Chronicles. 34:8-13).Each of Josiah's attempts for a spiritual reformation for Judah is recorded in II Kings 23. The information in this chapter informs us when Josiah implemented the restoration of the Temple, Hilkiah, (possibly Jeremiah's father – Jeremiah 1:2), found the lost Book of the Law given by Moses that had been lost so long most had forgotten about it. The Book of the Law contained the accounts of the blessings and curses that were to govern God's people, shared by Moses to the Jewish people, prior to their entering The Promise Land. This event is recorded in Deuteronomy 28-31. Moses divided the twelve tribes of Israel into two groups and stationed them on either side of a valley between Mt. Gerizim and Mt. Ebal. One side, comprised of six of the 12 tribes of Israel, was instructed to share a curse on God's people if they disobeyed God's requirements. The other six tribes, stationed on the other side of the valley, were instructed to share a blessing for obeying each of God's requirements. These curses and blessings were repeated back and forth across the valley until all of God's requirements were shared with God's people.

When the contents of the Book of the Law was read to king Josiah, he became so convicted of his sins and the sins of his nation, he began to tear his clothes, a sign of deep sorrow. Josiah sought more information on what Judah's disobedience to God's covenant meant and requested advice from Huldah, the prophetess. She confirmed that God was truthful. The people of Judah had forsaken God's covenant and His Word concerning Judah's judgment would be implemented. She also shared a word of reassurance for Josiah, informing him, because of his deep sorrow for the spiritual condition of his nation, God would withhold His judgment upon Judah until after his death (II Chronicles 34:14-33).

After Josiah received Huldah's comments, he called his people together in the house of the Lord and read the contents of the Book of the Law to them. He reminded his people of the covenants the Jewish people had made with God. He reminded them how those covenants had been broken. He made a covenant of his own that he and his people should follow in service to God.

At age 39, Josiah was killed by Pharaoh Necho, king of Egypt, at Megiddo and buried in his sepulcher in Jerusalem. Though Josiah was a godly king, his death occurred because of his disobedience to God's Word, as noted in II Chronicles 35:20-24.

> After all this, when Josiah had prepared the temple, Necho king of Egypt came up to fight against Charchemish by Euphrates: and Josiah went out against him. But he sent ambassadors to him, saying, What have I to do with thee, thou king of Judah? I come not against thee this day, but against the house wherewith I have war: for God commanded me to make haste: forbear thee from meddling with God, who is with me, that he destroy thee not. Nevertheless Josiah would not turn his face from him, but disguised himself, that he might fight with

> him, and hearkened not unto the words of Necho from the mouth of God, and came to fight in the valley of Megiddo. And the archers shot at king Josiah; and the king said to his servants, Have me away; for I am sore wounded. His servants therefore took him out of that chariot, and put him in the second chariot that he had; and they brought him to Jerusalem, and he died, and was buried in one of the sepulchers of his fathers. And all Judah and Jerusalem mourned for Josiah.

The people of Judah had convinced themselves the prophets who were prophesying of God's judgment upon Judah were wrong. Neither did the people of Judah place any confidence in what Huldah, the Prophetesses, had shared with Josiah concerning what would happen because God's people had refused to obey God's covenants. However, God had not forgotten His promise to judge Judah for the foolishness of Hezekiah (II Kings 20:13), and the sinfulness of Manasseh (II Kings 21:1-12).

> Notwithstanding the LORD turned not from the fierceness of his great wrath, wherewith his anger was kindled against Judah, because of all the provocations that Manasseh had provoked him withal. And the LORD said, I will remove Judah also out of my sight, as I have removed Israel, and will cast off this city Jerusalem which I have chosen, and the house of which I said, My name shall be there (II Kings 23:26-27).

As a side note, the Prophetess Huldah was Jeremiah's aunt. Jeremiah 32:7 reveals, "Behold, Hanameel the son of Shallum (the husband of Huldah--- II Chronicles 34:22), thine uncle shall come unto thee, saying, Buy thee my field that is in Anathoth: for the right of redemption is thine to buy it."

King Jehoahaz.

Jehoahaz (also known as Shallum), was twenty-three years old when he succeeded his father, Josiah, as king. He reigned only three months. Little is known about him other than he was taken prisoner by Pharaoh Necho and taken to Egypt, where he eventually died (II Kings 23:30-31). It would appear the people of Judah placed Jehoahaz on the throne. However, in that Egypt controlled Judah, Pharaoh Necho, the Egyptian king, removed Jehoahaz from the throne and replaced him with his older brother, Jehoiakim. One could speculate that the king of Egypt believed he could trust Jehoiakim to be more loyal to him than Jehoahaz. The Bible does not explain the removal of Jehoahaz as king. Scripture gives no evidence Jehoahaz was a godly king.

King Jehoiakim

II Kings 23:34 reveals, Pharaoh Necho replaced Jehoahaz's as king of Judah with his older brother, Eliakim, and changed his name to Jehoiakim. Jehoiakim was twenty-five years old when Pharo Necho placed him as king over Judah, and he served as king for eleven years. Five years into Jehoiakim's reign, the Babylonians defeated Egypt and permitted him to remain on the throne of Judah, but he became a puppet king for Babylon.

In Jeremiah 36, God commanded Jeremiah to remind Jehoiakim, and the people of Judah, of their sinfulness and their impending judgment. In that Jeremiah was in confinement, he dictated God's message to Baruch, his associate, and asked him to read his remarks in the House of the Lord. When Jehoiakim was informed of Jeremiah's message revealing the Babylonians would soon destroy Judah, he demanded to have Jeremiah's remarks read to him. After each page of Jeremiah's message was read to Jehoiakim, he would cast the pages into the fireplace to be burned.

God instructed Jeremiah to write another scroll and add more than was recorded in the scroll Jehoiakim burned. God not only instructed Jeremiah to inform Jehoiakim that Babylon would soon judge Judah, God also instructed Jeremiah to tell Jehoiakim he would soon die and how he would be buried. Note this in Jeremiah 36:27-32.

> Then the word of the LORD came to Jeremiah, after that the king had burned the roll, and the words which Baruch wrote at the mouth of Jeremiah, saying, Take thee again another roll, and write in it all the former words that were in the first roll, which Jehoiakim the king of Judah hath burned. And thou shalt say to Jehoiakim king of Judah, Thus saith the LORD; Thou hast burned this roll, saying, Why hast thou written therein, saying, The king of Babylon shall certainly come and destroy this land, and shall cause to cease from thence man and beast? Therefore thus saith the LORD of Jehoiakim king of Judah; He shall have none to sit upon the throne of David: and his dead body shall be cast out in the day to the heat, and in the night to the frost. And I will punish him and his seed and his servants for their iniquity; and I will

> bring upon them, and upon the inhabitants of Jerusalem, and upon the men of Judah, all the evil that I have pronounced against them; but they hearkened not. Then took Jeremiah another roll, and gave it to Baruch the scribe, the son of Neriah; who wrote therein from the mouth of Jeremiah all the words of the book which Jehoiakim king of Judah had burned in the fire: and there were added besides unto them many like words.

God sent the prophet Urijah to confront Jehoiakim for his sins and to warn him of God's impending judgment upon Judah. Both he and Jeremiah prophesied against Jerusalem and Judah, but when Jehoiakim heard Urijah's words, the king sought to have him executed. Urijah heard about Jehoiakim's plans for him and escaped to Egypt. Jehoiakim sent men to Egypt to capture Urijah. He had him brought back, killed, and his body cast into the graves of the common people (Jeremiah 26:20-23). Jehoiakim would have had Jeremiah killed, but God hid him and his associate, Baruch (Jeremiah 36:26).

In II Kings 24:1, reveals after three years as a puppet king for Babylon, Jehoiakim rebelled against Nebuchadnezzar. In his eleventh year, Nebuchadnezzar "... sent against him bands of the Chaldees, and bands of the Syrians, and bands of the Moabites, and bands of the children of Ammon, and sent them against Judah to destroy it, according to the word of the Lord, which he spake by his servant the prophet." Jeremiah tells us that Jehoiakim was killed during the eleventh year of his reign by either an engagement with some of these forces or at the hands of his own people. He did not receive the burial of a king, but was dragged away and "buried with the burial of an ass, beyond the gates of Jerusalem" (Jeremiah 22:18, 19; 36:30). Jehoiakim was a vicious and irreligious character (II Kings 2337; 24:9, II Chronicles 36:5).

King Jehoiachin

II Kings 24:6-7 shares that Jehoiachin, Jehoiakim's son, replaced Jehoiakim as king. Jehoiachin was eighteen years old when he became king. In II Kings 24:8 and II Chronicles 36:9, the influence of the Babylonians over Judah is noted by the fact Jehoiachin was permitted to serve as king of Judah for only three months and ten days before he was removed as king. "And Jehoiachin the king of Judah went out to the king of Babylon, he, and his mother, and his servants, and his princes, and his officers: and the king of Babylon took him in the eighth year of his reign" (II Kings 24:12). While the Judeans were denying God would judge them, it should have been evident that they were already under His judgment. Judah had suffered attacks from the Chaldees, the Syrians, the Moabites, and the Ammonites. Yet, they refused to believe God would judge them, or they deserved God's judgment.

Now, God would give Judah a real taste of what they could expect when the full force of His judgment would come. God would send the Babylonians to cease Jerusalem and remove some ten thousand of Judah's brightest and most productive people and carried them, and treasures of the house of the Lord, to Babylon. With all probability, some Judeans must have believed this was the judgment Jeremiah and the prophets had referred too. Little did the Judeans know this was only a small part of what God had in store for Judah? II Kings 24:10-17, records the first siege of Jerusalem.

At that time the servants of Nebuchadnezzar king of Babylon came up against Jerusalem, and the city was besieged. And Nebuchadnezzar king of Babylon came against the city, and his servants did besiege it. And Jehoiachin the king of Judah went out to the king of Babylon, he, and his mother, and his servants, and his princes, and his officers: and the king of Babylon took him in the eighth year of his reign. And he carried out thence all the treasures of the house of the LORD, and the treasures of the king's house, and cut in pieces all the vessels of gold which Solomon king of Israel had made in the temple of the LORD, as the LORD had said. And he carried away all Jerusalem, and all the princes, and all the mighty men of valour, even ten thousand captives, and all the craftsmen and smiths: none remained, save the poorest sort of the people of the land. And he carried away Jehoiachin to Babylon, and the king's mother, and the king's wives, and his officers, and the mighty of the land, those carried he into captivity from Jerusalem to Babylon. And all the men of might, even seven thousand, and craftsmen and smiths a thousand, all that were strong and apt for war, even them the king of Babylon brought captive to Babylon. And the king of Babylon made Mattaniah his father's brother king in his stead, and changed his name to Zedekiah.

King Zedekiah

Nebuchadnezzar, the king of Babylon, replaced Jehoiachin with his uncle, Mattaniah, and changed his name to Zedekiah. Zedekiah was twenty-one years old when he became king and served as king for eleven years before rebelling against Nebuchadnezzar. Zedekiah was evil. His only concern in life was himself. In Jeremiah chapter 34:1-3, as Nebuchadnezzar's army moved against Judah and the city of Jerusalem, God sent Jeremiah to Zedekiah with a prophetic message. Note what God asked Jeremiah to share with Zedekiah.

> The word which came unto Jeremiah from the Lord, when Nebuchadnezzar king of Babylon, and all his army, and all the kingdoms of the earth of his dominion, and all the people, fought against Jerusalem, and against all the cities thereof, saying, Thus saith the Lord, the God of Israel; Go and speak to Zedekiah king of Judah, and tell him, Thus saith the Lord; Behold, I will give this city into the hand of the king of Babylon, and he shall burn it with fire: And thou shalt not escape out of his hand, but shalt surely be taken, and delivered into his hand; and thine eyes shall behold the eyes of the king of Babylon, and he shall speak with thee mouth to mouth, and thou shalt go to Babylon.

Consider what the author of II Chronicles 36:12-21 said about Zedekiah and note how his lifestyle affected others.

> And he did that which was evil in the sight of the LORD his God, and humbled not himself before Jeremiah the prophet speaking from the mouth of the LORD. And he also rebelled against king Nebuchadnezzar, who had made him swear by God: but he stiffened his neck, and hardened his heart from turning unto the LORD God of Israel. Moreover all the chief of the priests, and the people, transgressed very much after all the abominations of the heathen; and polluted the house of the LORD which he had hallowed in Jerusalem. And the LORD God of their fathers sent to them by his messengers, rising up betimes, and sending; because he had compassion on his people, and on his dwelling place: But they mocked the messengers of God, and despised his words, and misused his prophets, until the wrath of the LORD arose against his people, till there was no remedy (2 Chronicles 36:12-16).

In verse sixteen, we note that God declared Judah incurable—they were without remedy.

> Therefore he brought upon them the king of the Chaldees, who slew their young men with the sword in the house of their sanctuary, and had no compassion upon young man or maiden, old man, or him that stooped for age: he gave them all into his hand. And all the vessels of the house of God, great and small, and the treasures of the house of the LORD, and the treasures of the king,

and of his princes; all these he brought to Babylon. And they burnt the house of God, and brake down the wall of Jerusalem, and burnt all the palaces thereof with fire, and destroyed all the goodly vessels thereof. And them that had escaped from the sword carried he away to Babylon; where they were servants to him and his sons until the reign of the kingdom of Persia: To fulfil the word of the LORD by the mouth of Jeremiah, until the land had enjoyed her sabbaths: for as long as she lay desolate she kept sabbath, to fulfil threescore and ten years.

God's judgment upon Judah was as severe as God had warned it would be. Before Israel entered into The Promise Land, the people of God were reminded by Moses, "... if thou shalt hearken diligently unto the voice of the LORD thy God, to observe and to do all his commandments which I command thee this day, that the LORD thy God will set thee on high above all nations of the earth" (Deuteronomy 28:1). They failed to observe God's command. Now, they would reap the consequences of their disobedience.

The majority of Judah's leadership was not of God's choosing, and often failed to observe what God required of them. This fact made Jeremiah's ministry even more difficult because the message he shared was against, not only Judah's political leaders, but also the leaders of those nations who either controlled Judah or who had attacked Judah. As Jeremiah shared his messages, he began with the assumption that all governments and nations were under the control of God. The basis of God's sovereignty, he noted, was God was the Creator of all things (Jeremiah 27:5). God was not only the God of His covenant people but of heaven and earth. No one was outside the realm of God's authority and command. This included all who opposed the nation of Judah.

With the exception of King Josiah, and the short time of Messiah's reign, after his conversion, the Kings of Judah who served during the time of Jeremiah's ministry were ungodly. This is evidenced by the fact that God did not appoint them and they did not honor and serve God by the requirements God outlined for the Kings of Israel (Deuteronomy 17:14-20). It is disappointing that the people of Judah raised no opposition or showed no serious concern their Kings were ungodly.

The spiritual leadership of Judah had forsaken God

Judah had progressively digressed into a spiritual quagmire. Judah needed a special message and God had a special messenger for them. God called Jeremiah. In that Jeremiah referred to himself as a child, has caused many to wonder how old he was. If Jeremiah was five when king Manasseh died, and seven when king Amon died and called to the ministry in the thirteenth year of Josiah, Jeremiah was twenty years old when God called him into the ministry. Jeremiah's ministry was active from the thirteenth year of Josiah, king of Judah (626 BC), until after the fall of Jerusalem and the destruction of Solomon's Temple in 587 BC. Jeremiah's ministry spanned more than forty years and the reign of five kings of Judah: Josiah, Jehoahaz, Jehoiakim, Jehoiachin, and Zedekiah. He was a contemporary with four of the Minor Prophets, Zephaniah, Habakkuk, Ezekiel, and Daniel. Jeremiah was raised in Anathoth, a little town located three miles up the road from Jerusalem (Jeremiah 1:1). He was the son of Hilkiah, who was a Hebrew priest at the time of King Josiah. It is believed by many theologians that his father is known for finding a lost copy of the Book of the law in the Temple in Jerusalem during the time king Josiah required the Temple be refurbished (II Kings 22:8).

Jeremiah was a faithful servant

No Prophet had a more difficult ministry than Jeremiah. God called him to minister in a time when most of the spiritual leaders in Judah were as corrupt and vile as the political leaders. Is it any wonder he was apprehensive when God called him to bring a message of judgment to his nation? Jeremiah was not knowledgeable of, nor the extent of, what God's call upon his life would entail. He did not feel he was qualified to share God's message. First, he used his age to excuse himself by saying, "...I am a child (Jeremiah 1:6). In excusing himself by his age, he was acknowledging his belief that he had neither the experience nor the ability to persuade those who were more knowledgeable, or more experienced, in life than he was. His second excuse involved fear (Jeremiah 1:8). He was afraid of what the people would physically do to him when he confronted their sinful living. He was also fearful of how they might perceive his message in that he was one of their own. A call to preach is not always embraced with open arms.

Knowing what Jeremiah would experience, God gave him His assurance of divine protection. God shared the following with Jeremiah:

> Thou therefore gird up thy loins, and arise, and speak unto them all that I command thee: be not dismayed at their faces, lest I confound thee before them. For, behold, I have made thee this day a defenced city, and an iron pillar, and brasen walls against the whole land, against the kings of Judah, against the princes thereof, against the

priests thereof, and against the people of the land. And they shall fight against thee; but they shall not prevail against thee; for I am with thee, saith the LORD, to deliver thee (Jeremiah 1:17-19).

Religious leaders often confronted Jeremiah because of the messages he shared. He preached against sin, naming sins by name. He faced isolation and rejection. He accused the religious leadership of lying, (Jeremiah 5:31), denying God would judge Judah, and "scattering the flock" (Jeremiah 23:1-2). He laid the responsibility for his people being captives of Babylon and refugees in Egypt at the feet of Judah's religious leaders. In Jeremiah 23:9, Jeremiah said his heart was broken because of the spiritual leadership of his nation. He summed up the depraved condition of the spiritual leadership of Judah in Jeremiah 5:31. He said, "The prophets prophesy falsely, and the priests bear rule by their means; and my people love to have it so: and what will ye do in the end thereof?" In most spiritual circles today Jeremiah would be considered too judgmental, dogmatic, dictatorial and politically incorrect.

In Jeremiah 23:10-4, Jeremiah said of the preachers of his day:

> For both prophet and priest are profane; yea, in my house have I found their wickedness, saith the LORD. Wherefore their way shall be unto them as slippery ways in the darkness: they shall be driven on, and fall therein: for I will bring evil upon them, even the year of their visitation, saith the LORD. And I have seen folly in the prophets of Samaria; they prophesied in Baal, and caused my people Israel to err. I have seen also in the

prophets of Jerusalem an horrible thing: they commit adultery, and walk in lies: they strengthen also the hands of evildoers, that none doth return from his wickedness; they are all of them unto me as Sodom, and the inhabitants thereof as Gomorrah. Therefore thus saith the Lord of hosts concerning the prophets; Behold, I will feed them with wormwood, and make them drink the water of gall: for from the prophets of Jerusalem is profaneness gone forth into all the land. Thus saith the Lord of hosts, Hearken not unto the words of the prophets that prophesy unto you: they make you vain: they speak a vision of their own heart, and not out of the mouth of the Lord. They say still unto them that despise me, The Lord hath said, Ye shall have peace; and they say unto every one that walketh after the imagination of his own heart, No evil shall come upon you. For who hath stood in the counsel of the Lord, and hath perceived and heard his word? who hath marked his word, and heard it? Behold, a whirlwind of the Lord is gone forth in fury, even a grievous whirlwind: it shall fall grievously upon the head of the wicked. The anger of the Lord shall not return, until he have executed, and till he have performed the thoughts of his heart: in the latter days ye shall consider it perfectly. I have not sent these prophets, yet they ran: I have not spoken to them, yet they prophesied. But if they had stood in my counsel, and had caused my people to hear my words, then they should have turned them from their evil way, and from the evil of their doings. Am I a God at hand, saith the LORD, and not a God afar off? Can any hide himself in secret places that I shall not see him? saith the LORD. Do not I fill heaven and earth? saith the LORD. I have heard what the prophets said, that prophesy lies in my name, saying, I have dreamed, I have dreamed. How long shall this be in the heart of the prophets that prophesy lies? yea, they are prophets of the deceit of their own heart; Which think to cause my people to forget my name by their dreams which they tell every man to his neighbour, as their fathers have forgotten my name for Baal. The prophet that hath a dream, let him tell a dream; and he that hath my word, let him speak my word faithfully. What is the chaff to the wheat? saith the LORD. Is not my word like as a fire? saith the LORD; and like a hammer that breaketh the rock in pieces? Therefore, behold, I am against the prophets, saith the LORD, that steal my words every one from his neighbour. Behold, I am against the prophets, saith the LORD, that use their tongues, and say, He saith. Behold, I am against them that prophesy false dreams, saith the LORD, and do tell them, and cause my people to err by their lies, and by their lightness; yet I sent them not, nor commanded them: therefore they shall not profit this people at all, saith the LORD. And when this people, or the prophet, or a priest, shall ask thee, saying,

What is the burden of the LORD? thou shalt then say unto them, What burden? I will even forsake you, saith the LORD. And as for the prophet, and the priest, and the people, that shall say, The burden of the LORD, I will even punish that man and his house. Thus shall ye say every one to his neighbour, and every one to his brother, What hath the LORD answered? and, What hath the LORD spoken? And the burden of the LORD shall ye mention no more: for every man's word shall be his burden; for ye have perverted the words of the living God, of the LORD of hosts our God. Thus shalt thou say to the prophet, What hath the LORD answered thee? and, What hath the LORD spoken? But since ye say, The burden of the LORD; therefore thus saith the LORD; Because ye say this word, The burden of the LORD, and I have sent unto you, saying, Ye shall not say, The burden of the LORD; Therefore, behold, I, even I, will utterly forget you, and I will forsake you, and the city that I gave you and your fathers, and cast you out of my presence: And I will bring an everlasting reproach upon you, and a perpetual shame, which shall not be forgotten.

In Jeremiah 19, God required Jeremiah to take a clay bottle, and ask some of the leading people and priests of Judah, to go with him to the valley of Hinnon and share His message with them. The valley of Hinnon was the place the people of Judah had sacrificed their children through burnt offerings to Baal, a false god, and the place where they currently burned their trash. Jeremiah's message was a warning of God's judgment for Judah.

> And say, Hear ye the word of the Lord, O kings of Judah, and inhabitants of Jerusalem; Thus saith the LORD of hosts, the God of Israel; Behold, I will bring evil upon this place, the which whosoever heareth, his ears shall tingle. Because they have forsaken me, and have estranged this place, and have burned incense in it unto other gods, whom neither they nor their fathers have known, nor the kings of Judah, and have filled this place with the blood of innocents; They have built also the high places of Baal, to burn their sons with fire for burnt offerings unto Baal, which I commanded not, nor spake it, neither came it into my mind: Therefore, behold, the days come, saith the LORD, that this place shall no more be called Tophet, nor The valley of the son of Hinnom, but The valley of slaughter. And I will make void the counsel of Judah and Jerusalem in this place; and I will cause them to fall by the sword before their enemies, and by the hands of them that seek their lives: and their carcases will I give to be meat for the fowls of the heaven, and for the beasts of the earth. And I will make this city desolate, and an hissing; every one that passeth thereby shall be astonished and hiss because of all the plagues thereof. And I will cause them to eat the flesh of their sons and the flesh of their daughters, and they shall eat every one the flesh of his friend

in the siege and straitness, wherewith their enemies, and they that seek their lives, shall straiten them (Jeremiah 19:3-9).

When he had shared this message, God further instructed Jeremiah:

> Then shalt thou break the bottle in the sight of the men that go with thee And shalt say unto them, Thus saith the LORD of hosts; Even so will I break this people and this city, as one breaketh a potter's vessel, that cannot be made whole again: and they shall bury them in Tophet, (the valley of Hennom),till there be no place to bury. Thus will I do unto this place, saith the LORD, and to the inhabitants thereof, and even make this city as Tophet: And the houses of Jerusalem, and the houses of the kings of Judah, shall be defiled as the place of Tophet, because of all the houses upon whose roofs they have burned incense unto all the host of heaven, and have poured out drink offerings unto other gods (Jeremiah 19: 10-14).

To be assured everyone heard his message, Jeremiah went into the court of the Lord's House and repeated his sermon (Jeremiah 19:15).

In Jeremiah 20, when Pashur, the Deputy High Priest, was informed of Jeremiah's message Jeremiah had shared in the valley of Hennom and repeated in the court of the House of the Lord, he was so angry with Jeremiah. He ordered him beaten (possible 39 lashes), and placed in the stocks just outside the House of the Lord to humiliate him. Jeremiah was not intimidated. He had a special message for Pashur from the Lord. This message is recorded Jeremiah 20:3-6.

> And it came to pass on the morrow, that Pashur brought forth Jeremiah out of the stocks. Then said Jeremiah unto him, The LORD hath not called thy name Pashur, but Magormissabib. (Fear on every side). For thus saith the LORD, Behold, I will make thee a terror to thyself, and to all thy friends: and they shall fall by the sword of their enemies, and thine eyes shall behold it: and I will give all Judah into the hand of the king of Babylon, and he shall carry them captive into Babylon, and shall slay them with the sword. Moreover I will deliver all the strength of this city, and all the labours thereof, and all the precious things thereof, and all the treasures of the kings of Judah will I give into the hand of their enemies, which shall spoil them, and take them, and carry them to Babylon. And thou, Pashur, and all that dwell in thine house shall go into captivity: and thou shalt come to Babylon, and there thou shalt die, and shalt be buried there, thou, and all thy friends, to whom thou hast prophesied lies.

In Jeremiah 27, God required Jeremiah to wear a yoke made of wood that signified the bondage God would soon require of Judah. Jeremiah was to wear this yoke and share his message with the ambassadors of the kings of Edom, Moab, the Ammonites, Tyrus, and Zidon who were in Jerusalem to see King Zedekiah.

In Jeremiah 28, Hananiah, the prophet, refused to believe Jeremiah's message and took the yoke off Jeremiah's neck, and broke it. Hananiah told the people that Jeremiah's message was wrong. God would remove them from the power of the Babylonians, all the captives would be returned from Babylon, and the vessels taken from the Temple restored within two years. Jeremiah 28:12-17, records Jeremiah's response to Hananiah.

> Then the word of the LORD came unto Jeremiah the prophet, after that Hananiah the prophet had broken the yoke from off the neck of the prophet Jeremiah, saying, Go and tell Hananiah, saying, Thus saith the LORD; Thou hast broken the yokes of wood; but thou shalt make for them yokes of iron. For thus saith the LORD of hosts, the God of Israel; I have put a yoke of iron upon the neck of all these nations, that they may serve Nebuchadnezzar king of Babylon; and they shall serve him: and I have given him the beasts of the field also. Then said the prophet Jeremiah unto Hananiah the prophet, Hear now, Hananiah; The LORD hath not sent thee; but thou makest this people to trust in a lie. Therefore thus saith the LORD; Behold, I will cast thee from off the face of the earth: this year thou shalt die, because thou hast taught rebellion against the LORD. So Hananiah the prophet died the same year in the seventh month.

The People of Judah were guilty of forsaking God

God promised Judah His judgement for the foolishness and sinfulness of Judah's leaders, but perhaps the greater sin was on behalf of the people of Judah who accepted their leaders' ungodliness, willingly. Amon was the only king murdered because of his ungodliness and the people of Judah rose up and murdered all of those who were involved in his death. The people of Judah were as corrupt as their leaders.

In Jeremiah 2:13, Jeremiah warned Judah for their sinful disobedience. He said, "For my people have committed two evils; they have forsaken me the fountain of living waters, and hewed them out cisterns, broken cisterns that can hold no water." Jeremiah's accusation must have seemed foolish to the Judeans, for they denied they had forsaken God and reminded Jeremiah that God's presence in the Temple would protect them (Jeremiah 7:4). Jeremiah did not say his people had forgotten God. His accusation was much worse. He said they had forsaken God. They had come to a point in their life, individually, and as a nation, they no longer believed God was important in supplying their needs. God sent Jeremiah to remind them who He was and the consequences for their disobedience. God instructed Jeremiah to inform them:

> Thine own wickedness shall correct thee, and thy backslidings shall reprove thee: know therefore and see that it is an evil thing and bitter, that thou hast forsaken the LORD thy God, and that my fear is not in thee, saith the Lord GOD of hosts. For of old time I have broken thy yoke, and burst thy bands; and thou saidst, I will not transgress; when upon every high hill and under every green tree thou wanderest, playing the harlot. Yet I

> had planted thee a noble vine, wholly a right seed: how then art thou turned into the degenerate plant of a strange vine unto me? (Jeremiah 2:19-21)

The second sin committed by the people of Judah that brought God's judgment was idol worship. In forsaking God, they turned their devotion to false gods, devised by their own hands. They turned away from the fountain of living water to a broken cistern, unable to hold the water of life. Throughout the Bible, water symbolizes God's Word, new life, cleansing, and the fulfillment of God's promises (Isaiah 12:3; 58:11; II Sam.22:17; John 4:14). The broken cistern is an illustration of Judah's failure to place their trust in the God who never fails. As obvious as their sinful actions were, they refused to acknowledge their sinfulness and denied God's accusation they had forsaken Him.

The people of Judah were guilty of Forsaking God's covenants

In Jeremiah 11, Jeremiah reminded the people of Judah they had forgotten the covenants of God.

> The word that came to Jeremiah from the LORD saying, Hear ye the words of this covenant, and speak unto the men of Judah, and to the inhabitants of Jerusalem; And say thou unto them, Thus saith the LORD God of Israel; Cursed be the man that obeyeth not the words of this covenant, Which I commanded your fathers in the day that I brought them forth out of the land of Egypt, from the iron furnace, saying, Obey my voice,

and do them, according to all which I command you: so shall ye be my people, and I will be your God: That I may perform the oath which I have sworn unto your fathers, to give them a land flowing with milk and honey, as it is this day. Then answered I, and said, So be it, O Lord. Then the Lord said unto me, Proclaim all these words in the cities of Judah, and in the streets of Jerusalem, saying, Hear ye the words of this covenant, and do them.⁷ For I earnestly protested unto your fathers in the day that I brought them up out of the land of Egypt, even unto this day, rising early and protesting, saying, Obey my voice. Yet they obeyed not, nor inclined their ear, but walked every one in the imagination of their evil heart: therefore I will bring upon them all the words of this covenant, which I commanded them to do: but they did them not. And the Lord said unto me, A conspiracy is found among the men of Judah, and among the inhabitants of Jerusalem. They are turned back to the iniquities of their forefathers, which refused to hear my words; and they went after other gods to serve them: the house of Israel and the house of Judah have broken my covenant which I made with their fathers. Therefore thus saith the Lord, Behold, I will bring evil upon them, which they shall not be able to escape; and though they shall cry unto me, I will not hearken unto them (Jeremiah 11:1-11).

This covenant occurred eight hundred years before Jeremiah was born. In Deuteronomy 28:1-68, God's covenant, and His requirements of the Jewish people to keep this covenant, was made just prior to their entering into The Promise Land. Moses led the Jewish people in a ceremony that involved each of the twelve tribes of Israel. Six tribes stood upon Mt. Ebal uttering curses on the children of Israel if they failed to obey God's Covenant. Six tribes stood on Mt. Gerizim who shared the blessing of this covenant for the people of Israel if they obeyed God's requirements. God used this experience to reemphasize His exclusive lordship over the Jewish people and the nation of Israel. By referring to God's covenants with Israel in his messages, Jeremiah reminded the people of Judah of their past, God's promises, provisions, and protection for them since their inception as a nation and the consequences for their disobedience.

What did God say would happen if His people failed to keep His covenants?

> But if ye will not hearken unto me, and will not do all these commandments; And if ye shall despise my statutes, or if your soul abhor my judgments, so that ye will not do all my commandments, but that ye break my covenant: I also will do this unto you; I will even appoint over you terror, consumption, and the burning ague, that shall consume the eyes, and cause sorrow of heart: and ye shall sow your seed in vain, for your enemies shall eat it. And I will set my face against you, and ye shall be slain before your enemies: they that hate you shall reign over you; and ye shall flee when none pursueth you. And if

ye will not yet for all this hearken unto me, then I will punish you seven times more for your sins. And I will break the pride of your power; and I will make your heaven as iron, and your earth as brass: And your strength shall be spent in vain: for your land shall not yield her increase, neither shall the trees of the land yield their fruits. And if ye walk contrary unto me, and will not hearken unto me; I will bring seven times more plagues upon you according to your sins. I will also send wild beasts among you, which shall rob you of your children, and destroy your cattle, and make you few in number; and your high ways shall be desolate. And if ye will not be reformed by me by these things, but will walk contrary unto me; Then will I also walk contrary unto you, and will punish you yet seven times for your sins. And I will bring a sword upon you, that shall avenge the quarrel of my covenant: and when ye are gathered together within your cities, I will send the pestilence among you; and ye shall be delivered into the hand of the enemy. And when I have broken the staff of your bread, ten women shall bake your bread in one oven, and they shall deliver you your bread again by weight: and ye shall eat, and not be satisfied. And if ye will not for all this hearken unto me, but walk contrary unto me; Then I will walk contrary unto you also in fury; and I, even I, will chastise you seven times for your sins. And ye shall eat the flesh of your sons, and the flesh of your daughters shall ye eat. And I will destroy your high places, and cut down your images, and cast your carcases upon the carcases of your idols, and my soul shall abhor you. And I will make your cities waste, and bring your sanctuaries unto desolation, and I will not smell the savour of your sweet odours. And I will bring the land into desolation: and your enemies which dwell therein shall be astonished at it. And I will scatter you among the heathen, and will draw out a sword after you: and your land shall be desolate, and your cities waste. Then shall the land enjoy her sabbaths, as long as it lieth desolate, and ye be in your enemies' land; even then shall the land rest, and enjoy her sabbaths. As long as it lieth desolate it shall rest; because it did not rest in your sabbaths, when ye dwelt upon it. And upon them that are left alive of you I will send a faintness into their hearts in the lands of their enemies; and the sound of a shaken leaf shall chase them; and they shall flee, as fleeing from a sword; and they shall fall when none pursueth. And they shall fall one upon another, as it were before a sword, when none pursueth: and ye shall have no power to stand before your enemies. And ye shall perish among the heathen, and the land of your enemies shall eat you up. And they that are left of you shall pine away in their iniquity in your enemies' lands; and also in the iniquities of their fathers shall they pine away with them. If they shall confess their iniquity, and the iniquity of their fathers, with their trespass which they trespassed against me, and that also they have walked contrary unto me; And that I also have walked contrary unto them, and have brought them into the land of their enemies; if then their uncircumcised hearts be humbled, and they then accept of the punishment of their iniquity: Then will I remember my covenant with Jacob, and also my covenant with Isaac, and also my covenant with Abraham will I remember; and I will remember the land. The land also shall be left of them, and shall enjoy her sabbaths, while she lieth desolate without them: and they shall accept of the punishment of their iniquity: because, even because they despised my judgments, and because their soul abhorred my statutes And yet for all that, when they be in the land of their enemies, I will not cast them away, neither will I abhor them, to destroy them utterly, and to break my covenant with them: for I am the LORD their God. But I will for their sakes remember the covenant of their ancestors, whom I brought forth out of the land of Egypt in the sight of the heathen, that I might be their God: I am the LORD. These are the statutes and judgments and laws, which the LORD made between him and the children of Israel in Mount Sinai by the hand of Moses (Leviticus 26:14-46).

How did the people of Judah respond when Jeremiah reminded them of their failure to keep God's covenants? Jeremiah answers this question in Jeremiah 2:31. The people of Judah responded by saying, "We are lords, we will no longer come unto thee." They became so spiritually depraved, they no longer cared what God thought or required of them. It would appear they assumed themselves wise enough to know what was best for them. They failed to remember King Solomon's instructions concerning wisdom. (Proverbs 8:1-36).

The People of Judah had forsaken God in their family life.

The commandments, statutes, and judgments God shared with His people prior to their entering the Promise Land was to be observed by His people and taught to their children. They had digressed to the point of saying, "There is no hope; but we will walk after our own devices, and we will every one do the imagination of his evil heart" (Jeremiah 8:12). As bad as the spiritual and social condition of Judah had become, there appeared to be no interest by Judean parents to teach their children about God. However, God's people were required to keep their families' focused on God. One of the things they were required to observe was the Shema. The Shema was a prayer of faith, acknowledging God as the only God who provided for and protected Israel. Devout Jews were to begin and close each day with the Shema, and teach this prayer to their children.

The author of Deuteronomy shares the instructions to Jewish parents concerning this prayer of faith in Deuteronomy 6:4-5.

> Now these are the commandments, the statutes, and the judgments, which the LORD your God commanded to teach you, that ye might do them in the land whither ye go to possess it: That thou mightest fear the LORD thy God, to keep all his statutes and

his commandments, which I command thee, thou, and thy son, and thy son's son, all the days of thy life; and that thy days may be prolonged. Hear therefore, O Israel, and observe to do it; that it may be well with thee, and that ye may increase mightily, as the Lord God of thy fathers hath promised thee, in the land that floweth with milk and honey. Hear, O Israel: The Lord our God is one Lord: And thou shalt love the Lord thy God with all thine heart, and with all thy soul, and with all thy might. And these words, which I command thee this day, shall be in thine heart: And thou shalt teach them diligently unto thy children, and shalt talk of them when thou sittest in thine house, and when thou walkest by the way, and when thou liest down, and when thou risest up. And thou shalt bind them for a sign upon thine hand, and they shall be as frontlets between thine eyes. And thou shalt write them upon the posts of thy house, and on thy gates. And it shall be, when the Lord thy God shall have brought thee into the land which he sware unto thy fathers, to Abraham, to Isaac, and to Jacob, to give thee great and goodly cities, which thou buildedst not, And houses full of all good things, which thou filledst not, and wells digged, which thou diggedst not, vineyards and olive trees, which thou plantedst not; when thou shalt have eaten and be full; Then beware lest thou forget the Lord, which brought thee forth out of the land of Egypt, from the house of bondage. Thou shalt fear the LORD thy God, and serve him, and shalt swear by his name. Ye shall not go after other gods, of the gods of the people which are round about you; (For the LORD thy God is a jealous God among you) lest the anger of the LORD thy God be kindled against thee, and destroy thee from off the face of the earth. Ye shall not tempt the LORD your God, as ye tempted him in Massah. Ye shall diligently keep the commandments of the LORD your God, and his testimonies, and his statutes, which he hath commanded thee. And thou shalt do that which is right and good in the sight of the LORD: that it may be well with thee, and that thou mayest go in and possess the good land which the LORD sware unto thy fathers. To cast out all thine enemies from before thee, as the LORD hath spoken. And when thy son asketh thee in time to come, saying, What mean the testimonies, and the statutes, and the judgments, which the LORD our God hath commanded you? Then thou shalt say unto thy son, We were Pharaoh's bondmen in Egypt; and the LORD brought us out of Egypt with a mighty hand: And the LORD shewed signs and wonders, great and sore, upon Egypt, upon Pharaoh, and upon all his household, before our eyes: And he brought us out from thence, that he might bring us in, to give us the land which he sware unto our fathers. And the LORD commanded us to do all these statutes, to fear the LORD our God, for our good always, that he might preserve us alive, as it is at this day. And it shall be our righteousness, if we observe to do all these commandments before the LORD our God, as he hath commanded us of the people which are round about you (Deuteronomy 6:4-14).

The People of Judah had forsaken God in their worship

Jeremiah shared his people worshipped as many gods as there were towns in Judah and streets in Jerusalem (Jeremiah 11:13). He also stated that there were gods being worshipped on ever "high hill and under ever green tree" (Jeremiah 2:20). His people had sunk so low spiritually; they were offering their children as burnt offerings (Jeremiah 19:5). They were guilty of committing sexual relationships with pagan prostitutes and calling it worship (Jeremiah 13:27). Most of their priests were more interested in advancing themselves rather than sharing God's Word (Jeremiah 2:8). Despite these acts of rebellion, the people of Judah denied they were sinful.

How does a Godly nation become so deceived that it refuses to accept spiritual truth? The acknowledgement of sin comes only when one understands and accepts the concept of sin. Sin goes deeper than missing the mark or falling short of God's will. Sin is a progressive act with no set boundaries. The first sinful act that occurred in the Garden of Eden demonstrates this as Satan deceived Eve into believing God was withholding His best from her (Genesis 3). As in that sin, all sin is conceived in the womb of deception, developed in disbelief, and birthed through disobedience.

God rejected the people of Judah's religious practices.

God's desire for the people of Judah was for a personal relationship with Him based upon faith and commitment. They chose to live as they pleased and believed all that was necessary for a right relationship with God was to perform their religious ceremonies. Jeremiah shared with them:

> Behold, ye trust in lying words that cannot profit. Will ye steal, murder, and commit adultery and sware falsely, And burn incense unto Baal, and walk after other gods whom ye know not; And come and stand before me in my house, which is called by my name, and say, We are delivered to do all these abominations (Jeremiah 7:8-10).

God's message assured the people of Judah, despite their observance of religious ceremonies, He was mindful of their continuous sinful practices. "For though thou wash thee with nitre, and take thee much soap, yet thine iniquity is marked before me, saith the Lord GOD" (Jeremiah 2:22). He informs them that their religious ceremonies, like salt or soap, were not a justifiable cleansing agent that would cleans their sinfulness.

When they asked, "How can you say we are polluted?" Jeremiah responded, "Look and see." He used two illustrations to prove his point. Jeremiah said, "You remind me of a camel on the desert floor and a wild female burro in heat." No doubt confused by his statement they would have asked, "What do you mean? How are we like a camel and a female burro?" Jeremiah would have responded, "If you want to know where the camel has been, look over the camel's shoulder. Every time the camel puts its hoof down in the sand, it leaves a print. Looking back across the desert you can see the camel's prints in the sand and know where that camel has been. He is encouraging the people of Judah to re-examine their life by asking themselves, "Where have I been and what have I been doing?"

As a young man, I heard a sermon entitled, "If Things Could Talk." The preacher said, "If your shoes could talk, they could tell me where you have been. Some of your shoes might tell me you were at the Club Saturday night. Some of your shoes might tell me you are a frequent patron at the local liquor store. If your shoes could talk, would you be willing to come up front and permit your shoes to tell us where you have been lately?" Jeremiah uses a similar analogy to illustrate the sinfulness of the people of Judah.

In Jeremiah's analogy, if you want to know where the camel is going, get behind the camel and look. If the camel does not change course, it will continue to go in the same direction. Judah was going in the wrong direction spiritually. They demonstrated no willingness to change directions. Jeremiah's illustration is designed to help his people see their sinfulness, and to help them understand their need to change course.

As they begin a self-examination, Jeremiah shifts gears and becomes extremely graphic. He says, "Not only do you remind me of a camel on the desert floor, you also remind me of a wild female burro in heat." He describes a burro with an overwhelming desire to be satisfied. Her only focus was for a male burro, any male burro, to satisfy her desire. Jeremiah then says, "You say you are not sinful? You are like this burro. You are consumed by your desire for your sinful-indulgence. You are as stubborn as this burro, unwilling to focus on anything or anyone except what satisfies you." No doubt, Jeremiah would have said, "How can you say we are sinful?"

Despite the fact the people of Judah had forsaken God, shunned His sovereignty, violated His covenants, forsaken Him in their family life, and settled for religion, they refused to believe they were sinful. Judah's sinfulness had reached the point of callousness. In Jeremiah 2:26, we read, "As the thief is ashamed when he is found, so is the house of Israel ashamed; they, their kings, their princes, and their priests, and their prophets." Accused for their sinful behavior was the only remorse they felt.

Judges 19, records the most egregious acts of callousness recorded in the Bible. This chapter tells the story of a Levite who lived in the remote mountains of Ephraim. He had taken a concubine who became unfaithful to him, committed adultery, left him, and returned to her father's home in Bethlehem Judah. After waiting four months, he decided to travel to Bethlehem with the hope of bringing his concubine home. When he arrived in Bethlehem there was reconciliation between he and his concubine, but rather than returning home, his father-in-law encouraged him to stay and fellowship with him. On the afternoon of the fifth day, the Levite, his concubine, his servant and the two mules began their journey home. As they passed by Jebus, his servant requested they spend the night there. The Levite refused, fearing it was too dangerous to stay in a pagan city and chose to continue on to Gibeah, a city of the Benjamites. As they arrived in Gibeah, the sun was setting. When no one invited them into their home, he and his servant began to prepare to spend the night in the city square. Finally, an old man, a fellow Ephramite who had come to Gibeah looking for work, came in out of the field and invited them to spend the night with him.

After their evening meal, a group of homosexual men gathered outside the old man's home desiring to know the Levite sexually. At first, the old man expressed his disgust for their request. The old man offered his daughter for their sexual pleasure. When they refused to take his daughter, the old man gave them the Levite's concubine. They took her and abused her all night long.

The Levite's callousness was demonstrated by saying and doing nothing to prevent his concubine from the torture she would endure. While he was content to lay down and spend the night in restful peace, she was enduring a night of torture that would claim her life. She was released at the breaking of the dawn; she made her way back to the old man's house, lay down at the door, and died. When the Levite arose from sleep, he expressed his appreciation to the old man for his hospitality. In leaving to return home he tripped over his concubine's body lying at the door of the old man's house and said to her in a calloused tone, "Up, and let's be going." Not realizing she was dead, his only concern was she was delaying him.

The story of this Levite's callousness toward his concubine is akin to Judah's callousness toward God. The Levite was no more concerned about his reconciliation with his concubine than the people of Judah were with their reconciliation with God. It took the Levite four months before he was willing to go after his Concubine. He was content to allow the old man to offer his daughter to those men. He said nothing when the old man gave those men his concubine. He was only concerned with his own welfare. Content, he lay down and went to sleep while his concubine was being abused. He expressed his anger and frustration toward her for delaying his return home when he discovered her lying at the old man's door the following morning. Both the Levite and the people of Judah would deny any culpability for their actions. Despite what the Levite and the people of Judah saw and heard, they chose to do nothing. However, in defense of the Levite, the death of his concubine affected him enough that he challenged the Jewish people to condemn the Benjamites for their homosexuality and those in Gibeah who would not condemn their actions. God's judgment against the Benjamites was severe (Judges 20).

This analogy is evidenced by what Jeremiah records in Jeremiah 6:13-18

> For from the least of them even unto the greatest of them every one is given to covetousness; and from the prophet even unto the priest every one dealeth falsely. They have healed also the hurt of the daughter of my people slightly, saying, Peace, peace; when there is no peace. Were they ashamed when they had committed abomination? nay, they were not at all ashamed, neither could they blush: therefore they shall fall among them that fall: at the time that I visit them they shall be cast down, saith the Lord. Thus saith the Lord, Stand ye in the ways, and see, and ask for the old paths, where is the good way, and walk therein, and ye shall find rest for your souls. But they said, We will not walk therein. Also I set watchmen over you, saying, Hearken to the sound of the trumpet. But they said, We will not hearken. Therefore hear, ye nations, and know, O congregation, what is among them.

The people of Judah had become so calloused against God, God shared with Jeremiah, "Therefore thou shalt speak all these words unto them; but they will not hearken to thee: thou shalt also call unto them; but they will not answer thee." The people of Judah had become so spiritually depraved, God instructed Jeremiah not to pray for them (Jeremiah 7:16; 11:14; 14:11).

What was Jeremiah's message?

It is of interest to note God's call for Jeremiah involved sharing His message with nations and kingdoms. God was not appointing him to become a ruler over these nations and kingdoms. Jeremiah was to represent God as His prophet. The Bible does not inform us which nations or kingdoms Jeremiah was to share God's message. However, it is apparent from reading the book of Jeremiah; his message is applicable for all nations and kingdoms. His message included Babylon and Egypt, for these nations were in control of Judah during Jeremiah's ministry. We can also conclude God's message through Jeremiah had a special meaning for the people of Judah. His message had six parts, four negative and two positive. "See, I have this day set thee over the nations and over the kingdoms, to root out, and to pull down, and to destroy, and to throw down, to build, and to plant (Jeremiah 1:10).

God commissioned Jeremiah to "root out, pull down, destroy, and throw down: What do these requirements imply? In that the Judeans believed they were not sinful, and God would not judge them, God's message was to illustrate their sinfulness. God's message called Judah to repentance and reminded them of the consequences for their disobedience if they did not repent. Note God's message to the Judeans in Jeremiah 2:19-37.

> Thine own wickedness shall correct thee, and thy backslidings shall reprove thee: know therefore and see that it is an evil thing and bitter, that thou hast forsaken the LORD thy God, and that my fear is not in thee, saith the Lord GOD of hosts. For of old time I have broken thy yoke, and burst thy bands; and thou saidst, I will not transgress; when upon every high hill and under every green tree thou wanderest, playing the harlot.[1] Yet I had planted thee a noble vine, wholly a right seed: how then art thou turned into

the degenerate plant of a strange vine unto me? For though thou wash thee with nitre, and take thee much soap, yet thine iniquity is marked before me, saith the Lord God. How canst thou say, I am not polluted, I have not gone after Baalim? see thy way in the valley, know what thou hast done: thou art a swift dromedary traversing her ways; A wild ass used to the wilderness, that snuffeth up the wind at her pleasure; in her occasion who can turn her away? all they that seek her will not weary themselves; in her month they shall find her. Withhold thy foot from being unshod, and thy throat from thirst: but thou saidst, There is no hope: no; for I have loved strangers, and after them will I go. As the thief is ashamed when he is found, so is the house of Israel ashamed; they, their kings, their princes, and their priests, and their prophets. Saying to a stock, Thou art my father; and to a stone, Thou hast brought me forth: for they have turned their back unto me, and not their face: but in the time of their trouble they will say, Arise, and save us. But where are thy gods that thou hast made thee? let them arise, if they can save thee in the time of thy trouble: for according to the number of thy cities are thy gods, O Judah. Wherefore will ye plead with me? ye all have transgressed against me, saith the Lord. In vain have I smitten your children; they received no correction: your own sword hath devoured your prophets, like a destroying lion. O generation, see ye the word of the

Lord. Have I been a wilderness unto Israel? a land of darkness? wherefore say my people, We are lords; we will come no more unto thee? Can a maid forget her ornaments, or a bride her attire? yet my people have forgotten me days without number. Why trimmest thou thy way to seek love? therefore hast thou also taught the wicked ones thy ways. Also in thy skirts is found the blood of the souls of the poor innocents: I have not found it by secret search, but upon all these. Yet thou sayest, Because I am innocent, surely his anger shall turn from me. Behold, I will plead with thee, because thou sayest, I have not sinned. Why gaddest thou about so much to change thy way? thou also shalt be ashamed of Egypt, as thou wast ashamed of Assyria. Yea, thou shalt go forth from him, and thine hands upon thine head: for the Lord hath rejected thy confidences, and thou shalt not prosper in them.

God's message through Jeremiah was pungent. He called their sin into account by name and reminded them of God's correction despite the fact they no longer referenced God's Lordship over them. Jeremiah reminded them of God's attempts for them to repent. They would soon discover their sinfulness was evil and their sinfulness would have a bitter impact upon them and their children.

God judges Judah

Throughout the ministry of Jeremiah, he forewarned the people of Judah of God's judgment because of their sinfulness and their unwillingness to repent. In the thirty-ninth chapter of Jeremiah, Jeremiah records the fulfillment of God's promise to judge Judah.

> In the ninth year of Zedekiah king of Judah, in the tenth month, came Nebuchadnezzar king of Babylon and all his army against Jerusalem, and they besieged it. And in the eleventh year of Zedekiah, in the fourth month, the ninth day of the month, the city was broken up. And all the princes of the king of Babylon came in, and sat in the middle gate, even Nergalsharezer, Samgarnebo, Sarsechim, Rabsaris, Nergalsharezer, Rabmag, with all the residue of the princes of the king of Babylon. And it came to pass, that when Zedekiah the king of Judah saw them, and all the men of war, then they fled, and went forth out of the city by night, by the way of the king's garden, by the gate betwixt the two walls: and he went out the way of the plain. But the Chaldeans' army pursued after them, and overtook Zedekiah in the plains of Jericho: and when they had taken him, they brought him up to Nebuchadnezzar king of Babylon to Riblah in the land of Hamath, where he gave judgment upon him. Then the king of Babylon slew the sons of Zedekiah in Riblah before his eyes: also the king of Babylon slew all the nobles of Judah. Moreover he put out Zedekiah's eyes, and bound him with chains, to carry him to Babylon. And the Chaldeans burned the king's house, and the houses of

the people, with fire, and brake down the walls of Jerusalem. Then Nebuzaradan the captain of the guard carried away captive into Babylon the remnant of the people that remained in the city, and those that fell away, that fell to him, with the rest of the people that remained. But Nebuzaradan the captain of the guard left of the poor of the people, which had nothing, in the land of Judah, and gave them vineyards and fields at the same time. Now Nebuchadrezzar king of Babylon gave charge concerning Jeremiah to Nebuzaradan the captain of the guard, saying, Take him, and look well to him, and do him no harm; but do unto him even as he shall say unto thee. So Nebuzaradan the captain of the guard sent, and Nebushasban, Rabsaris, and Nergalsharezer, Rabmag, and all the king of Babylon's princes; Even they sent, and took Jeremiah out of the court of the prison, and committed him unto Gedaliah the son of Ahikam the son of Shaphan, that he should carry him home: so he dwelt among the people. Now the word of the LORD came unto Jeremiah, while he was shut up in the court of the prison, saying, Go and speak to Ebedmelech the Ethiopian, saying, Thus saith the LORD of hosts, the God of Israel; Behold, I will bring my words upon this city for evil, and not for good; and they shall be accomplished in that day before thee.[7] But I will deliver thee in that day, saith the LORD: and thou shalt not be given into the hand of the men of whom thou art afraid. For I will surely deliver thee, and thou shalt not fall by the sword, but thy life shall be for a prey unto thee: because thou hast put thy trust in me, saith the LORD (Jeremiah 39:1-18).

This event is also recorded in II Kings 25:1-30. God sent Nebuchadnezzar's Babylonian army against Judah. As the Babylonians approached Jerusalem, they conquered all of the smaller cities. Many of the people of those cities fled into Jerusalem seeking shelter and safety. A siege was built around the walls of Jerusalem preventing anyone from coming into or leaving Jerusalem. This was done to starve those in Jerusalem into submission and surrender. Jeremiah, in Lamentations 2:11, records the success of this siege. We are told of little children crying for food to eat; in Lamentations 2:20, of mothers who were starving, murdered their infant children and ate them (Lamentations 4:10). Conditions in Jerusalem became unbearable.

Jerusalem's economy was depleted. Businesses were closed. Money to purchase needed items became useless, for there was nothing to purchase. Those who had been a part of the elite society now huddled in the streets with the poorest of the poor begging for something to eat. In addition to all the horrors endured within the city of Jerusalem, the anticipation of the Babylonian army breaking through the walls and slaughtering them was an even greater threat. Day after day, for eighteen months, God's judgment became a reality. Without doubt, they often pondered messages they had heard Jeremiah preach. If they had only heeded what he shared with them, they would not be enduring these awful events.

In II Kings 25:3-7, as the famine grew worse, Zedekiah, his sons and his soldiers broke a section from the wall and sought to escape by night. When the Babylonian troops discovered they had escaped, they pursued them. The soldiers deserted their King and scattered, believing it would be more difficult for the Babylonians to find and capture them. Zedekiah and his sons were captured in the planes of Jericho, twenty miles from Jerusalem. They had reached the place where Israel had first entered into the Promise Land and where Israel had won her first victory as the walls of Jericho had fallen by the power of God. Having reached this area, most Jews considered holy, Zedekiah and his sons probably assumed they were safe. Zedekiah was experiencing Jeremiah's prophecy concerning him, as recorded in Jeremiah 34:1-3.

The Babylonians captured Zedekiah and his sons and brought them to Riblah for judgment. Zedekiah was made to watch as each of his sons, and some of his Court officials, were murdered. These murders would be the last thing he would ever see, for his eyes were gouged out. This fulfilled the prophecy of Ezekiel regarding Zedekiah shortly before the fall of Jerusalem, as recorded in Ezekiel 12:13. "My net also will I spread upon him, and he shall be taken in my snare: and I will bring him to Babylon to the land of the Chaldeans; yet shall he not see it, though he shall die there." Zedekiah became a prisoner in Babylon and remained a prisoner for thirty-seven years, until Nebuchadnezzar died and Merodach, his son, became King (II Kings 25:27). Merodach released Zedekiah and "spoke kindly to him" (2 Kings 25:28), and gave him a place at Merodach's table for the remainder of Zedekiah's life (2 Kings 25:29).

In II Kings 25:8-10, the Babylonians broke through the walls of Jerusalem and destroyed the city. The people of Judah had refused to believe God's message through Jeremiah. Now, they stood in disbelief and watched as their homes, their city and the House of God was being burned.

The walls surrounding Jerusalem that had provided protection from their enemies for many years were being torn down. What they were watching was beyond their wildest imagination.

> And in the fifth month, on the seventh day of the month, which is the nineteenth year of king Nebuchadnezzar king of Babylon, came Nebuzaradan, captain of the guard, a servant of the king of Babylon, unto Jerusalem: And he burnt the house of the LORD, and the king's house, and all the houses of Jerusalem, and every great man's house burnt he with fire. And all the army of the Chaldees, that were with the captain of the guard, brake down the walls of Jerusalem round about.

In II Kings 25:11-17, we are told who Nebuchadnezzar removed from Jerusalem and who he permitted to stay and why. We also are told how the Temple of the Lord was pillaged and what items from the Temple were removed and carried to Babylon for their material value. Now, God's judgment had become a reality.

> Now the rest of the people that were left in the city, and the fugitives that fell away to the king of Babylon, with the remnant of the multitude, did Nebuzaradan the captain of the guard carry away. But the captain of the guard left of the poor of the land to be vinedressers and husbandmen. And the pillars of brass that were in the house of the LORD, and the bases, and the Brasen

Sea that was in the house of the LORD, did the Chaldees break in pieces, and carried the brass of them to Babylon. And the pots, and the shovels, and the snuffers, and the spoons, and all the vessels of brass wherewith they ministered, took they away. And the firepans, and the bowls, and such things as were of gold, in gold, and of silver, in silver, the captain of the guard took away. The two pillars, one sea, and the bases which Solomon had made for the house of the LORD; the brass of all these vessels was without weight. The height of the one pillar was eighteen cubits, and the chapter upon it was brass: and the height of the chapter three cubits; and the wreathen work, and pomegranates upon the chapter round about, all of brass: and like unto these had the second pillar with wreathen work.

Jeremiah mourns over his Nation

Jeremiah was not exempt from all the suffering that took place in Jerusalem during the siege by the Babylonians. Yet, his daily provisions were better than most. This was because of God's promise to Jeremiah to protect and provide for him (Jeremiah 1:18-19). The siege around the city of Jerusalem shut off the food supply. As many in Jerusalem were starving and becoming angry because of their incrassation by the Babylonian Army, God used King Zedekiah to provide Jeremiah with safety from the people and a fresh loaf of bread each day (Jeremiah 37:21).

The book of Lamentations, written after the fall of Jerusalem, gives an understanding of what it was like during and after the days of Jerusalem's capture by the Babylonians. In each of the five poems that comprise the book of Lamentations, Jeremiah paints a vivid picture of God's judgment against Judah and Jerusalem. He reveals what he saw and felt as he walked through the city of Jerusalem during and after God's judgment upon his people. He identifies himself as crushed by his loneliness. He remembers the Jerusalem that once was. He remembers the city that God loved and the Temple where God had met with His people. He remembers the cries of little children for something to eat when no food was available. In his mind, he could see those mothers who murdered their children and ate them. He saw the bodies of the priest who opposed his message, and the bodies of city leaders who refused to assist him, all lying in the street having starved to death. Everywhere he looks, he sees death and ruin. Houses burned, the Temple destroyed, and the walls around Jerusalem torn down.

In the midst of his sorrow, Jeremiah cries out to God asking why he had to endure such hardship. He records his plea to God in Lamentations 3:1-18.

> I AM the man that hath seen affliction by the rod of his wrath. He hath led me, and brought me into darkness, but not into light. Surely against me is he turned; he turneth his hand against me all the day. My flesh and my skin hath he made old; he hath broken my bones. He hath builded against me, and compassed me with gall and travail. He hath set me in dark places, as they that be dead of old. He hath hedged me about, that I cannot get out: he hath made my chain heavy. Also when I cry and shout, he shutteth out my prayer. He hath

inclosed my ways with hewn stone, he hath made my paths crooked. He was unto me as a bear lying in wait, and as a lion in secret places. He hath turned aside my ways, and pulled me in pieces: he hath made me desolate. He hath bent his bow, and set me as a mark for the arrow. He hath caused the arrows of his quiver to enter into my reins. I was a derision to all my people; and their song all the day. He hath filled me with bitterness, he hath made me drunken with wormwood. He hath also broken my teeth with gravel stones, he hath covered me with ashes. And thou hast removed my soul far off from peace: I forgat prosperity. And I said, My strength and my hope is perished from the LORD:

In these verses, we hear the heart of a shepherd who loved his flock. Jeremiah's heart is broken because of Judah's refusal to hear and heed God's warnings against their sinful living. We hear Jeremiah's frustration and anger leveled at himself for not being able to persuade his people to change. In the midst of his hurt, he cries out to God, asking, "God why? Why did you choose me to be your spokesperson? Why did you choose me to endure all that I have endured? God, what could I have said or done differently that would have prevented your judgment on my nation. God, I am crushed. I feel as though you have forsaken me. I pray, but you do not hear my prayers. I have become a bitter person. I am angry and do not know who to be angry with or even how to vent my anger. My people hate me. I am void of peace. I am tired. God, why?"

As Jeremiah laments his plight, like a true shepherd, he reminds himself of who God is. In Lamentations 3:22-26, Jeremiah says:

> It is of the LORD's mercies that we are not consumed, because his compassions fail not. They are new every morning: great is thy faithfulness. The LORD is my portion, saith my soul; therefore will I hope in him. The LORD is good unto them that wait for him, to the soul that seeketh him.

Chapter 3

HAS AMERICA GONE TOO FAR?

We often hear the statement made, "America is a Christian nation." Is this an accurate statement? When considering the spiritual decline of America over the past twenty-five to thirty years, the evidence makes it difficult to justify the trustworthiness of this statement. (45) Consider the following:

- Eighty percent of Americans are not actively involved in church.
- Only twenty-four percent of Americans believe the Bible is the literal Word of God.
- Sixty-four percent of Americans believe God accepts the worship of all religions
- Twenty-five percent of "Christian" Americans believe in reincarnation.
- Seventy percent of Americans believe many religions provide a path to eternal life.
- Sixty-four percent of Americans believe everyone will go to heaven when they die.
- Only thirty-two percent of Americans believe hell is a real place. (46)

The people of Judah were guilty of forsaking God and settling for a broken cistern that could not support the truth of God's Word. Americans have followed the descending path of Judah. Many Americans, like the people of Judah, have placed God and sin into their own mold. For many, sin has become what they perceive sin to be, not what sin is. For this group of people, God is a God of convenience. Paul addresses this in Romans 1:18-32.

> For the wrath of God is revealed from heaven against all ungodliness and unrighteousness of men, who hold the truth in unrighteousness; Because that which may be known of God is manifest in them; for God hath shewed it unto them. For the invisible things of him from the creation of the world are clearly seen, being understood by the things that are made, even his eternal power and Godhead; so that they are without excuse: Because that, when they knew God, they glorified him not as God, neither were thankful; but became vain in their imaginations, and their foolish heart was darkened. Professing themselves to be wise, they became fools, And changed the glory of the incorruptible God into an image made like to corruptible man, and to birds, and fourfooted beasts, and creeping things. Wherefore God also gave them up to uncleanness through the lusts of their own hearts, to dishonour their own bodies between themselves: Who changed the truth of God into a lie, and worshipped and served the creature more than the Creator,

who is blessed for ever. Amen. For this cause God gave them up unto vile affections: for even their women did change the natural use into that which is against nature: And likewise also the men, leaving the natural use of the woman, burned in their lust one toward another; men with men working that which is unseemly, and receiving in themselves that recompence of their error which was meet. And even as they did not like to retain God in their knowledge, God gave them over to a reprobate mind, to do those things which are not convenient; Being filled with all unrighteousness, fornication, wickedness, covetousness, maliciousness; full of envy, murder, debate, deceit, malignity; whisperers, Backbiters, haters of God, despiteful, proud, boasters, inventors of evil things, disobedient to parents, Without understanding, covenantbreakers, without natural affection, implacable, unmerciful: Who knowing the judgment of God, that they which commit such things are worthy of death, not only do the same, but have pleasure in them that do them.

Contrary to the opinion of many, America no longer remains a Christian nation. (47) It takes more than a founding document to make America a Christian nation. America is spiritually sick and the sickness is fever-hot. Many in the church today are practical atheist. They have not denied there is a God; they simply chose to live as though God does not exist. In II Timothy 3:5, Paul tells us that, in the last days, many in the church will have a form of godliness, but they will deny the power thereof. The spiritual depravity of America is evidenced by its movies, its music, and the message from many pulpits that makes a mockery of Christianity. Vulgarity has become the language of the day. The flagrant disregard of the murdering of thousands of children in abortion clinics across American each day is beyond shameful. Sexual perversion has becoming accepted. While America becomes more sinful, the messages from many pulpits remain silent on many subjects the Bible condemns. As you examine the remainder of this chapter, ask yourself, "Has America Gone Too Far?"

America's political leadership has forsaken God

Sharing the condition of the political leadership of America is a difficult task. What makes this so difficult is the deception of the media. With all the distortion and lies the liberal media shares, it is difficult to know what truth is and what is untrue. The media has an ideology based in liberalism and socialism. If a President supports a liberal or a socialist view in his agenda, he and his Administration are favored. If a President supports a conservative view in his agenda, he and his Administration are vilified. With rare exception, only a few percentage points separate the elections of America's Presidents. This indicates the people of America are equally divided between having a conservative or socialist view.

Jeremiah's ministry lasted approximately forty years, and under the leadership of five kings. Examining the Presidents of America since 1974 will provide a time of forty-three years that will enable us to compare America's political leadership to the political leadership of Judah during the days of Jeremiah. Is there any comparison between the political and spiritual leadership of America today to the political and spiritual leadership of Judah during the days of Jeremiah? The Bible clearly illustrates most of the kings of Judah were corrupt and void of a commitment to God during the days of Jeremiah. An examination of America's presidents from President Richard Nixon to the presidency of President Obama reveals the political leadership of America, with few exceptions, was no better spiritually than the political leadership of Judah during the days of Jeremiah. James 4:17, says, "Therefore to him that knoweth to do good, and doeth it not, to him it is sin,"

Before the inauguration of each president, he is required to take an "Oath of Office." The oath requires of him to swear, "I do solemnly swear (or affirm) that I will faithfully execute the Office of President of the United States, and will to the best of my ability, preserve, protect and defend the Constitution of the United States." Though not required, the statement "So help me God" has been used by every president since Lincoln to conclude his oath. The Bible is most often used in the taking of the Oath of Office, yet it is not required. On September 5, 1901, Theodore Roosevelt became president upon the assassination of William McKinley who was shot by Leon Czolgosz in Buffalo, New York. No Bible was used when he took the oath of office. Both John Quincy Adams and Franklin Pierce swore on a book of law, with the intention they were swearing on the Constitution. Lyndon B. Johnson was sworn in on a Roman Catholic Missal, a book containing the prayers and rites used by Priest in celebrating Mass.

The Oath the President takes is a promise to uphold the Constitution. The Constitution is the supreme law of the United States, guarantying certain basic rights for its citizens. Using God's name and swearing to an oath of office by placing one's hand on the Bible does not mean the one who is taking the oath, is a believer and follower of God, rather the procedure has become merely a formality.

President Richard Nixon:

President Nixon is the only president who resigned from the office of president. Two years into his second term, he resigned rather than to be impeached because of his participation in the Watergate Scandal. The Watergate Scandal began on the morning of June 17, 1972, when several burglars were arrested in the office of the Democratic National Committee, located in the Watergate complex of buildings in Washington, D.C. (48) Those arrested were connected to President Richard Nixon's re-election campaign. They were caught wiretapping phones and stealing documents. President Nixon went to extreme lengths to cover up the crime. In August of 1974, after his conspiracy was confirmed, he resigned. The Watergate Scandal changed American politics forever, leading many Americans to question their leaders and think more critically about the presidency. Though a Quaker, President Nixon demonstrated little evidence of a spiritual commitment. In his private life, he was without doubt one of the most vulgar speaking presidents. This fact can be verified because he recorded much of what he said in the Oval Office.

President Gerald Ford:

President Ford is the only president to serve as president and vice president of the United States that was not elected to either office. (49) He was appointed to become vice president by President Nixon after Spiro Agnew resigned from office, pleading no contest to a charge of federal income tax evasion in exchange for dropping charges against him for political corruption.

Upon becoming President, one of President Ford's first acts was to grant President Nixon a pardon for all offenses. He also gave amnesty for those who evaded the draft or deserted during the Vietnam War. The majority of Americans did not appreciate these two acts. When asked about his relationship to Christ, he often said his faith was a private matter. There is no evidence that he advocated or promoted Christianity through his time as President.

President Jimmy Carter:

Before becoming president, he was a peanut farmer, governor of Georgia, and known by many as a Southern Baptist Sunday School teacher in the Maranatha Baptist Church, located in his home town of Plains, Georgia. (50) He is a supporter and works with Habitat for Humanity, an organization started by Millard and Linda Fuller.

Despite his good deeds, as a Democrat, he embraces the Democrat platform that supports abortion, same-sex marriages and the LBGT (lesbian, bisexual, gay, transgender) agenda, all of which the Bible clearly denounces. President Carter, in an interview with Beliefnet.com, stated his belief that there is salvation outside of faith in Christ. He further stated he believed all persons will be saved. Jesus said, in John 14:6, "I am the way, the truth, and the life: no man cometh unto the Father, but by me." He has been a constant critic of Israel. In Genesis 12:3, the Lord said in the covenant He made with Abraham, "I will bless those who bless you, and I will curse him who curses you; and in you all the families of the earth shall be blessed." This relates, not only to a people (the Jews), but it also relates to a Nation, Israel.

The kings of Judah, during the days of Jeremiah, also refused to believe the truths of God's Word.

President Ronald Reagan:

Before becoming president, President Reagan had been a radio sports announcer, an actor, and governor of California. (51) From the beginning of President Reagan's administration, he demonstrated an opposition to abortion and the support for mandatory prayer in the public schools. He gave strong evidence of his belief that Jesus was the Messiah, the Son of God. Michael Reagan, President Reagan's son, said at President Reagan's funeral, "On a flight from Washington to California in 1988, my father told me, about his love of God, and his love of Christ as his Savior." Michael Reagan also said at his father's funeral, "When Dad closed his eyes that is when I realized the gift that he gave to me – the gift that he was going to be with his Lord and Savior, Jesus Christ." (52)

President Reagan was responsible for helping to reform Israel's economic crisis. In 1985, when Israel's inflation rate reached 445%, he led the Congress to grant Israel $1.5 billion in emergency assistance to deal with their economic problem. Under President Reagan, Israel began to receive $3 billion annually in foreign aid, and the financial support to Israel continues. President Reagan has been given credit for ending the Cold War with the Soviet Union. He was a strong conservative, Christian, and brilliant leader. He would be akin to King Hezekiah. He established the norm for what a president should be.

President George H. W. Bush

Prior to serving as president, he served as vice president under President Ronald Reagan. Throughout his campaign, he promised a "kinder, gentler nation." He also emphasized he would reduce the federal deficit. Neither of these was accomplished. Recently, with sexual accusations being made against politicians, eight women have accused President H.W. Bush with sexual harassment. (53)

He supported Planned Parenthood and was pro-choice until he became Ronald Ragan's vice-presidential candidate. When Israeli government officials asked for a ten billion dollar loan to help settle Russian Jewish immigrants into Israel, President George W. H. Bush delayed the request to be assured the money would not be used to build houses on the West Bank, land claimed by the Palestinians. Many believe George H.W. Bush lost his attempt for a second term as president because he offended Jewish voters across America over his hard line view against Israel. Like so many other presidents, President H.W. Bush did not publically promote Christianity through his office as president.

President Bill Clinton:

Some believe President Bill Clinton is one of the best-liked presidents in America history. Others view him as "Slick Willie." This nickname refers to his immoral character that he and his wife, Hillary, sought to conceal from the public. (54) Both he and his wife, Hillary, are rumored to be involved in numerous unlawful acts. (55) He was accused of having a sexual encounter with Gennifer Flowers while serving as governor of Arkansas as he campaigned for the Presidency in 1992. He denied the accusation. However, in January 1998, in sworn testimony, in his deposition in the

Paula Jones sexual harassment case, he acknowledged his sexual relationship with Gennifer Flowers. He said it was a onetime encounter. She testified the relationship lasted for some twelve years. Other women have publicly accused him of sexual misconduct. Juanita Broaddrick accused him of raping her in 1978; Kathleen Willey accused him of groping her in 1993; and Paula Jones accused him of exposing himself to her. (56) President Clinton was impeached on charges of perjury and obstruction of justice for his lies about his sexual relationship with Monica Lewinsky. On February 12, 1999, after his five-week impeachment trial ended, the Senate voted to acquit him on both articles of impeachment. (57) Every Democratic and ten Republicans voted for acquittal. There have been many rumors of sexual misconduct made against him over the years.

President Clinton's position on same sex marriages went from opposition to promotion. To settle questions about his understanding of abortion, President Clinton went to his pastor, Rev. W. O. Vaught, pastor of Immanuel Baptist Church in Little Rock, Arkansas, and asked him what the Bible had to say about abortion. President Clinton said, Rev. Vaught, shared with him that in the original Hebrew the word, 'personhood' came from the words translated "to breathe life into." Reportedly, Rev. Vaught told President Clinton life began at birth and one could not say definitively, based on Scripture, abortion was murder. In all his comments about abortion thereafter, President Clinton has shared what Rev. Vaught shared with him. President Clinton was a supporter of abortion. (58) He voted twice in favor of Partial-birth abortion a procedure in which the abortionist pulls a living baby, feet-first out of the womb and into the birth canal (vagina), except for the head, which the abortionist purposely keeps lodged just inside the cervix. The abortionist punctures the base of the baby's skull with a surgical instrument. He or she then inserts a tube into the wound, and removes the baby's brain with a powerful suction machine. This causes the skull to collapse, after which the abortionist completes the delivery of the now-dead baby.

Isaiah 59:7 is applicable to every politician who supports abortion. Isaiah shares, "Their feet run to evil, and they hasten to shed innocent blood; their thoughts are thoughts of iniquity, devastation and destruction are in their highways." God's judgment upon Judah came, in part, because Manasseh was guilty of shedding innocent blood, which involved the murder of the righteous and the sacrifice of children to the god, Moloch. II Kings 21:16 says, "Moreover Manasseh shed innocent blood very much, till he had filled Jerusalem from one end to another; beside his sin wherewith he made Judah to sin, in doing that which was evil in the sight of the LORD."

President Clinton's giving North Korea more than four billion dollars to disband and dismantle their nuclear weapons program has proven to be an ultimate failure. (59) The North Korean leadership used the four billion dollars to build nuclear weapons that pose a nuclear threat to many countries. King Hezekiah's foolish decision to show the Babylonians his military strength was no more foolish than President Clinton's act in providing North Korea the money necessary to build their nuclear weapons (Isaiah 39). Though President Clinton claimed to be a Christian, his actions have caused many to doubt the validity of his claim.

President George W. Bush

President George W. Bush is the son of President George H. W. Bush. Before becoming President, George W. Bush was the governor of Texas. (60) His opponent in the

2000 presidential election was Al Gore. It was reported that Al Gore won the popular vote, receiving 50,996,582 votes, George Bush received 50,456,062 votes and Ralph Nader received 2,882,955 votes. There was a discrepancy with the votes from Florida. The Supreme Court ruled George Bush had won the State of Florida on December 12, 2000, by a 5 to 4 majority vote. The 911 attack on the World Trade Center and the Iraq War are two major events that occurred during his presidency.

President George W. Bush had a strong pro-life stance, consistently opposing abortion while supporting parental notification for minor girls who wanted an abortion. Unlike his father, he was a friend to Israel. The liberal media vilified him, like other conservative presidents. One of his first acts as president was to invite some thirty leading clergy and other religious leaders to the First Baptist Church in Austin, Texas to discuss his commitment to public funding of religious ministries. Unlike his father, President George Bush was proactive concerning Christianity.

President Barack Hussein Obama:

To say President Obama was the first African-American to become the president of the United States is not a truthful statement. He is a Mulatto. President Obama's mother, Stanley Ann Dunham was a Caucasian American anthropologist, who specialized in the economic anthropology and rural development of Indonesia. His father was a Kenyan, Barack Hussein Obama, Sr., a Kenyan senior governmental economist. His mother and father divorced in 1964 and his mother remarried in 1965 to Lolo Soetoro, an Indonesian. Between the ages of 6 to 10, President Obama was raised in the home of his Muslim stepfather. At age 10, he began to live with his grandparents in Hawaii. (61)

Many doubt he was born in America. There are many who doubt his statement that he attended Columbia University. Professor Henry Graff taught at Columbia University from 1946 to 1991. He said in a recent interview,

> I taught at Columbia for 46 years, I taught every significant American politician that ever studied at Columbia. I know them all. I'm proud of them all. Between American History and Diplomatic History, one way or another, they all had to come through my classes. Not Obama. I never had a student with that name in any of my classes. I never met him, never saw him, and never heard of him. None of the other Columbia professors knew him either. (62)

There are numerous allegations made against President Obama and his administration during his tenure as president. (63) America's debt doubled under President Obama's presidency, giving him the worst economic record of any President in America's history. During his administration, America witnessed a new low in social issues. Same sex marriages became the law of the land. He directed all American schools to make all bathrooms transgender or face lawsuits and the potential loss of federal funding. President Obama supported the Muslim Brotherhood, a terrorist organization, placing several Muslim Brotherhood individuals into positions in his administration. (64) On several occasions, he proved he was no friend to Israel. He used taxpayer's money to campaign against Benjamin Netanyahu, as he campaigned to be the Prime Minister of Israel. (65)

God gave Israel guidelines for their national leaders to follow. Examining the kings who served Judah during the days of Jeremiah, there is little evidence to indicate the people of Judah were concerned about the spiritual depth of their kings. Any nation that desires the blessings of God should heed God's principles for their leaders. Professing a Christian and demonstrating Christlikeness as a national leader are two different issues. When America's political leaders support social issues the Bible condemns, one is to believe they are more concerned in political correctness than spiritual correctness. Their actions brings a reproach on the will of God tor our nation.

Who controls America?

As the people of Judah were denying being captured and carried into captivity, they were already under the control of the Egyptians, or the Babylonians. Ten years prior to the fall of Judah, Nebuchadnezzar's troops captured Jerusalem and removed thousands of Judah's best and brightest, and carried them into captivity in Babylon.

Americans might argue, "America is not under the control of anyone or any group." Yet, an argument can be made that an oligarchy rules America. An oligarchy is a form of government in which power is vested in a dominant class or a small group that exercises control over its people. Is there a group of people who formulate and implement America's policies and practices? Some believe there is, and have given this group the name, "the shadow government." Others call this group "the deep state," which refers to a group of influential members of government agencies and the military. Some Americans believe there is a group of people, outside the government and the military, who are manipulating the government and social policy of America. (66)

Those who comprise this group and its members are not known. However, informed American's are beginning to understand that this group exist, and the various means they will use to accomplish their objective. They use America's banks, the liberal news media, the judicial system, and federal judges to promote their agenda. They use politicians, democrats, and republicans. Evidence, presented of late, also indicates they have used the Internal Revenue, the Federal Bureau of Investigation, the Central Intelligence Agency, and other government entities. They use lies, half-truths, and character assassination to discredit anyone who opposes their agenda. To convert America into socialism and bring America into globalism, this group must destroy America's Christian culture and the Second Amendment. (67)

The forces for a One World Government are not new. John F. Hylan, a former mayor of New York City, was quoted in the New York Times, on March 26, 1922, as saying:

> The real menace of our Republic is the invisible government, which like a giant octopus sprawls its slimy legs over our cities, states and nation... The little coterie of powerful international bankers virtually run the United States government for their own selfish purposes. They practically control both parties ... and control the majority of the newspapers and magazines in this country. They use the columns of these papers to club into submission or drive out of office public officials who refuse to do the bidding of the powerful corrupt cliques which compose the invisible government. It operates under cover of a self-created screen [and] seizes our executive officers, legislative bodies, schools,

courts, newspapers and every agency created for the public protection.

On June 10, 1932, Congressman Louis T. McFadden delivered a speech before the House of Representatives, saying:

> Mr. Chairman, we have in this country one of the most corrupt institutions the world has ever known. I refer to the Federal Reserve Board and the Federal Reserve Banks. The Federal Reserve Board, a Government board, has cheated the Government of the United States and the people of the United States out of enough money to pay the national debt...Mr. Chairman, when the Federal Reserve act was passed, the people of the United States did not perceive that a world system was being set up here... and that this country was to supply financial power to an international superstate — a superstate controlled by international bankers and international industrialists acting together to enslave the world for their own pleasure. (68)

Did the election of Donald Trump change this trend?

The opinion of many Americans is that the election of President Donald Trump in 2016 declared, "Enough is enough" and resulted in an outsider of politics to become president. The news media, members of the Democratic Party and many in the Republican Party have opposed him from the outset of his announcement to seek the office of the president. It is becoming evident that the Obama Administration used the FBI, the CIA, and the Department of Justice to delegitimize Donald Trump's candidacy and presidency. Despite the fact he has accomplished more to assist Christianity than any president has in modern history, many religious leaders reject him and his presidency. Will his election change the spiritual condition of America? King Josiah sought to change the spiritual condition of Judah and failed. Unfortunately, Donald Trump will fare no better than King Josiah did. It must be remembered one's righteousness is the result of a personal relationship to God. Neither King Josiah nor President Donald Trump can dictate another's personal relationship with God. The corruption in America will continue.

Some believe President Trump is hated because he is an outsider to Washington's political elite. Others believe it is because he is seeking to "drain the swamp," a term that implies he will expose and attempt to remove the corruption created by politicians in Washington, DC. Yet, others believe he is hated because of his stance against bringing America into globalism.

The fulfillment of a One World Government was advanced by the approval of "Agenda 21," that was presented to the Earth Summit for the UN, which was held in Rio de Janeiro, Brazil, in 1992. President George H.W. Bush endorsed this agenda and President's Bill Clinton and Barack Obama supported the idea. President Trump's opposition of a One World Government has not only angered those in Washington who support this idea, his election as president has angered Satan.

The Bible reveals that, in the last days, Satan will establish his false Christ, who will become the leader of the world. The antichrist will be exalted, and given authority over every nation (Revelation 13:7). He will rule the world for seven years. The first half of this seven years period will be the Tribulation. The Great Tribulation, which refers to the more intense second half of the seven-year period, is noted in Matthew 24:21, Daniel 12:1, Zephaniah 1:15, and Jeremiah 30:7. These days will be a time of sorrow and sadness, akin to nothing the world has ever experienced before. Paul speaks of these days in II Thessalonians 2:3-4. He says, "Let no man deceive you by any means: for that day shall not come, except there come a falling away first, and that man of sin be revealed, the son of perdition Who opposeth and exalteth himself above all that is called God, or that is worshipped; so that he as God sitteth in the temple of God, shewing himself that he is God."

Spiritual leaders have forsaken God

The decline of America's churches over the past twenty-five to thirty years reveals a greater decline than the decline churches in America experienced during the sixties and seventies. In an attempt to reverse the effects of this decline, religious leaders have sought to formulate new ideas for worship. The new ideas include:

- Wearing different attire rather than the traditional suit of days past.
- Contemporary music, to attract the youth and young adults.
- Omitting Sunday evening services to support family time.
- Sermons that are shorter, less controversial, and more upbeat.
- The removal of training programs.
- More emphasis on church structured excursions.
- Making pastors CEO's.

- Making worship services more attractive to the lost.
- Selecting church leaders that are not spiritually qualified.

None of these attempts is having a positive impact on reversing the decline that churches are experiencing. The Bible reveals, prior to the return of Christ, sinfulness will become more intense. Paul reveals, "And because iniquity shall abound, the love of many shall wax cold" (Matthew 24:12).

Over the past twenty-five to thirty years, messages from many pulpits across America have greatly emphasized God's unconditional love for humanity, almost to the exclusion of God's message on sin and judgment. Contrary to popular preaching, God's love has conditions. If God's love were unconditional toward the sinner, no one would be lost. It must also be understood, God has conditions for Cristian's to have fellowship with Him, as indicated by Matthew 16:24, "Then said Jesus unto his disciples, If any man will come after me, let him deny himself, and take up his cross, and follow me." No one can be a follower of Christ who does not meet these conditions. We enter into heaven by observing the conditions of faith in the finished work of Christ on the cross. Listen carefully to John 14:21, "Whoever has my commands and obeys them, he is the one who loves me. He who loves me will be loved by my Father, and I too will love and show myself to him." Thus, keeping God's commandments is a condition required by God. Before one can become a Christian, they must die to self and submit themselves to allow Christ to live in and through them. For one to receive the blessings of the Christian life, they must be obedient to God's commands.

The message from many pulpits emphasizes God's love for the sinner with very little emphases on the consequences of sin. The Bible reveals God loves the sinner. However, the refusal of sinners to respond to the truth of God's Word, God's grace, and God's forgiveness, has its consequences. This is a message seldom heard from preachers today. Altering the gospel negatively affects individuals, families, and nations.

Spiritual leaders hinder the cause of God when they alter the Word of God. There are spiritual leaders who are at the forefront of sanctioning homosexuality, abortion, same-sex-marriages, and other issues the Bible condemns. These spiritual leaders are creating a negative impact upon the Word of God and leading the uninformed down a dark path. The prophet Micah's depiction of Judah draws a striking parallel to America today. Micah said, "The leaders judge for a bribe, priest teach for a price, and prophets tell fortunes for money. Yet they lean upon the Lord and say, 'Is not the Lord among us,'" (Malachi 3:11).

Does God ever reach a point that He hates the sinner? Consider the following verses.

> **Psalms 11:5** – The Lord trieth the righteous: but the wicked and him that loveth violence his soul hateth.
> **Leviticus 20:23** – And ye shall not walk in the manners of the nation, which I cast out before you: for they committed all these things, and therefore I abhorred them.
> **Proverbs 6:16-19** – These six things doeth the Lord hate: yea seven are an abomination unto him: A proud look, a lying tongue, and hands that shed innocent blood, A heart that deviseth wicked imaginations, feet that be swift in running to mischief, A false witness that speaketh

lies, and he that soweth discord among brethren.

Hosea 9:15 – All their wickedness is in Gilgal: for there I hated them: for the wickedness of their doings I will drive them out of mine house, I will love them no more: all their princes are revolters.

John 3:36 – He that believeth on the Son hath everlasting life: and he that believeth not the Son shall not see life; but the wrath of God abideth on him.

In America today, we have judges who use the judicial system to force their unchristian agenda upon the American people. Same-sex-marriages, was sanctioned by the Justices of the Supreme Court. (69) This act by the Supreme Court violated God's requirements for a marriage and thousands of years of common practice. In 2012, at the Democratic Convention in Charlotte, North Carolina, many of the delegates became upset that the mention of God was placed in their Convention's Platform and began to boo. Liberal professors are using the educational system to instill their antichristian ideology. Today, many consider prayer and the Bible "hate speech." Christianity has become a target for many present-day comedians. Across America, crosses from college chapels, local parks, and mountaintops are being removed that have been in place for many years. Religious leaders are currently sanctioning sexual perversion. Church leadership supports and hires those who violate God's requirements for holy living. Indeed, the silence from pulpits across America concerning these and other issues that are destroying America clearly indicates many of America's spiritual leadership have forsaken God.

God is forsaken in our homes

If you doubt families in America have forsaken God, consider this, most marriages in America are non-scriptural. Marriage is a divine institution ordained of God and requires two believers, a man, and a woman. In Ezra, chapters 9 and 10, Ezra reveals God's displeasure for His people marring unbelievers. In Ezra 10:10-11, we read, "And Ezra the priest stood up, and said unto them, Ye have transgressed, and have taken strange wives, to increase the trespass of Israel. Now therefore make confession unto the LORD God of your fathers, and do his pleasure: and separate yourselves from the people of the land, and from the strange wives.'" Paul addresses this same issue in II Corinthians 6:14-16:

> Be ye not unequally yoked together with unbelievers: for what fellowship hath righteousness with unrighteousness? and what communion hath light with darkness? And what concord hath Christ with Belial? or what part hath he that believeth with an infidel? And what agreement hath the temple of God with idols? For ye are the temple of the living God; as God hath said, I will dwell in them, and walk in them; and I will be their God, and they shall be my people.

Paul is issuing a command to those in Corinth to stop joining themselves together in marriage with unbelievers. The accomplishment of God's will is impossible for a couple unequally yoked together. Righteousness and unrighteousness cannot coexist. Neither can light and darkness, God and Satan, or the worship of God and Idols. When a Christian marries a non-Christian, it is impossible for such a union to glorify God, accomplish His will, or raise children by biblical standards. Standing before a preacher sharing a vow to a God you do not know with an intent to raise children as God intended without the aid of the Holy Spirit to assist, is a fallacy. A non-Scriptural marriage is an act of forsaking God.

American families forsake God when parents are unable or unwilling to fulfill Proverbs 22:6, "Train up a child in the way he should go, and when he is old he will not depart from it." It should not come as a surprise that youth violence has become a national concern. Juvenile arrest is on the rise, and the majority of youth have no church affiliation.

The decline in church attendance and baptisms is another indication families have forsaken God. The largest attended event on any given Sunday morning, in most cities, is the local youth, sports field. The Bible declares hell is a real place and all who die not knowing Christ as their Savior will spend eternity in hell. It is one thing to believe about God, it is another to believe God. For many, the God of the Bible has been forsaken and replaced with a god formulated out of personal satisfaction. As a nation, America, like Judah, is saying, "We are lords we will no longer come unto you" (Jeremiah 2:31).

Does it matter how we live?

God's message through Jeremiah was, in part, a reminder to the people of Judah that their lifestyle, and the lifestyle of their ancestors, was one of the reasons for God's judgment. Note Jeremiah 16:10-12:

> And it shall come to pass, when thou shalt shew this people all these words and they

shall say unto thee, wherefore hath the LORD pronounced all this great evil against us? Or what is our iniquity? Or what is our sin that we have committed against the LORD our God? Then shalt thou say unto them, Because your fathers have forsaken me, saith the LORD, and have walked after other gods, and have served them, and have worshipped them, and have forsaken me, and have not kept my law; And ye have done worse than your fathers; for, behold, ye walk every one after the imagination of his evil heart, that they may not hearken unto me:

In verse 13, God declares His judgment for the way the people of Judah were living. If God would judge Judah for their sinfulness, He will also judge America.

God is forsaken in schools

Proverbs 9:10, says, "The fear of the LORD is the beginning of wisdom: and the knowledge of the holy is understanding." To fear God means more than respecting God or holding Him in high esteem. These two factors are important; however, one fears God when he trusts His Word and lives his life to prevent the consequences of disobeying God's Word. Paul shared with the church at Corinth, "Knowing therefore the terror of the Lord, we persuade men..." One of the greatest problems America has today is the absence of a fear of God.

It is obvious parents of the children of Judah did not teach their children about God. Their children observed their parent's actions and comments and learned what their parents believed should be worshipped. Having forsaken God, the people of Judah worshipped as many gods as there were towns in Judah (Jeremiah 11:13), and all the gods they erected on every high hill and under every greet tree (Jeremiah 3:13). Children of America's parents are being taught what to worship in the same manner.

For many years in America, schools began each morning with the Pledge of Allegiance and the reading of a passage from the Bible, or the reciting of a prayer. As America's demographics have changed so have America's customs. School boards began to file lawsuits claiming forcing students to use the name of God was unconstitutional because it violated the Establishment Clause of the First Amendment. (70)

Each of the fifty states has a group of individuals who are responsible for the general supervision of all educational activities within that state. Those who are responsible for the supervision of education in our schools are known as Trusties, a Board of Regents, or a Board of Governors. In the State of New York, they are known as the Board of Regents. This Board is comprised of seventeen members, and elected by the State Legislature and serve a five-year term. In the early 1950's, the Board of Regents in New York recommended the school boards of New York adopt a resolution calling for a prayer to be recited each morning as the students began their day in school. The prayer was a very simple prayer that acknowledged God and the student's dependence upon Him. The prayer asked God for His blessing upon four groups of people: the students, their parents, their teachers and America. The students recited this prayer each morning. "Almighty God, we acknowledge our dependence upon Thee, and we beg Thy blessings upon us, our parents, our teachers, and our country. Amen." School board officials believed they were not violating any student's individual rights, because they included a provision in which students could opt out of the prayer with their parent's permission.

Steven Engel, who was Jewish, took exception to the prayer, believing the prayer was unconstitutional. Mr. Engel joined with fellow parents, Monroe Lerner, Lenore Lyons, Dan Lichtenstein, and Larry Ross, and sued the president of New York's Board of Regence, William Vitale, to stop the practice of this prayer on behalf of his children. (71) He argued the law violated the Establishment Clause of the First Amendment, as made applicable to the states through the Due Process Clause of the Fourteenth Amendment. The New York's courts ruled in favor of the Board of Regence. However, the case came before the Supreme Court on April 3, 1962. On June 25, 1962, the Supreme Court ruled against the Board of Regence and in favor of Mr. Vitale and his four friends. Hugo Black wrote the opinion for the majority argument of the Supreme Court stating, "The decision of the Board of Regence to encourage recitation of a prayer was inconsistent with the Establishment Clause." There are two clauses in the First Amendment that concern the relationship of government to religion: the Establishment Clause and the Free Exercise Clause. The two clauses state that Congress shall make no law respecting an establishment of religion, or prohibiting the free exercise thereof.

Justice Potter Stewart was the only Justice on the Supreme Court who voted in favor of the New York Board of Regence. He argued, "The majority of the Supreme Court Justices had misapplied a great constitutional principle and he could not understand how an 'official religion' is established by letting those who want to say a prayer, say it." He further stated, "On the contrary, I think to deny the wish of these school children to join in reciting this prayer is to deny them the opportunity of sharing in the spiritual heritage of our Nation."

Following the Supreme Court ruling in the Engle vs Vitale case in 1962 more suits have been adjudicated by the Supreme Court to remove the Bible, God, and prayer from schools. (72)

- * In 1963, in the case of the District of Abington Township vs. Schempp, the Supreme Court struck down voluntary Bible readings and recitation of the Lord's Prayer in public schools. (73)
- * In 1980, the Supreme Court in the Stone vs. Graham Case ruled against a Kentucky law that required the posting of the Ten Commandments in all public school classrooms. (74)
- * In the 1980's and 1990's, some states enacted "a moment of silence" or "a minute of silence" laws with the intent of allowing students to conduct private prayer or spiritual reflection in the classroom. Although the Supreme Court found an early Alabama law unconstitutional in Wallace v. Jaffrey (1985), subsequent laws have generally survived legal challenges.
- * In 1992, the Supreme Court in the Lee vs. Weisman Case ruled that school officials violated the First Amendment by inviting clergy to give an invocation and a benediction at a public high school graduation. (75)
- * In 2000, the Supreme Court in the Santa Fe Independent School District vs. Doe Case, ruled against a Texas school district policy of facilitating prayers over the public address system at football games and against holding elections to choose the student to deliver the prayer.(76)

If you picked up a US history book from the late 1960's, you would be presented with a very different picture of American history than is being presented to schoolchildren and students in colleges and universities today. (77) American history is being both rewritten and removed from school curriculum. The liberal bias that seeks to shape America's history is persistent in their antichristian agenda. The new American history, presented to students and mocked by those in our colleges and universities, is not only shameful it is dangerous. It is shameful because it is not true. It is dangerous because it establishes a faulty foundation on which to build a strong and productive future.

What is the purpose behind the altering of America's history? It is to Manipulate. Psychological manipulation is a type of social influence that aims to change the behavior or perception of others through abusive, deceptive, or underhanded tactics. Today, educators are teaching that America is a nation anchored on racism and bigotry. The days of slavery and all the horrors that occurred associated with slavery should be taught to prevent such an event from ever occurring again. However, the days of slavery should be taught in context. Martin Luther King, and others, should be given the credit they deserve for advancing race relationships in America. The mistreatment of the American Indian should also be taught. No group of people have been mistreated more than the American Indian. Even today, Indians are living on reservations, of which many do not have adequate plumbing or running water in their homes.

A more concise answer to this question of "Why is American History being manipulated?" is to be found in observing the social changes that have taken place in America over the past twenty-five to thirty years. Each of the changes is a strategic, orchestrated, manipulation to advance the agenda of a group of people operating from the shadows to bring America into a One World Government system. A focal point of this agenda is an all-out attack against Christianity.

God is forsaken in churches

Satan was behind the sinfulness that brought about God's judgment upon Judah. Satan is behind the sinfulness of American today. Satan has an uncanny ability to transform himself into whatever and to use whomever he deems necessary to accomplish his objective. To prevent humanity from knowing who he is, and what he seeks to do, he attacks the mind. Every form of communication Satan uses to deceive humanity is channeled through the mind. Therefore, Satan attacks man's mind with lies, half-truths, distortions, gimmicks, and schemes. Satan uses each of these to prevent humanity from coming to know God as their Savior, and hindering the saved from serving God.

Satan's objective is to defeat God and God's redemptive plan for man. He does this by attacking the Word of God, the church, Christians, preachers, Bible teachers, biblical marriages, and God's intended purpose for a man and a woman. It is not by accident Satan lurks in the shadows. He knows that if he can distort man's view of who he is or prevent humanity from accepting the fact he exist, his attacks will be more effective. He is the master of deception.

When one begins a conversation about the church, the first thought that comes to mind is a building; however, the church is not a building. The church building is a place where the church gathers to worship at appointed times. The redeemed of God are the church. Satan attacks the true church by attempting to distort the world's opinion of the church. He does this by drawing attention to the weaknesses of church members and diverting attention away from true worship by the church.

Satan has deceived many into believing the church is beyond his reach. Those who believe this must disregard Paul's teachings to the church at Thessalonica. In II Thessalonians 2:3-4, Paul said, "Let no man deceive you by any means: for that day shall not come, except there come a falling away first, and that man of sin be revealed, the son of perdition: who opposeth and exalteth himself above all that is called God, or that is worshipped; so that he as God sitteth in the temple of God, shewing himself that he is God."

Satan's influence upon the church today is causing many to forsake God. The decline of the church is alarming. Many churches have removed their Sunday evening services, training programs, and revival services. If an event, other than entertainment, cost money or requires commitment and attendance, it will suffer in most churches. Satan knows the value of Godly pastors, staff members, and church leaders for the success of a church. He will do all he can to destroy Godly leadership. He will deceive pulpit committees and churches into calling pastors and staff members who are not God's choice for a church. Satan leads nominating committees to place individuals into leadership positions within churches who have neither the spiritual qualifications or the desire to do God's will. Satan knows when a pastor, a staff member, or church leader is not in his proper place of service, and living as they should, they cannot accomplish God's will.

The gospel declares the birth, life, death, resurrection, and return of Christ. The gospel is the good news that God's love and grace is sufficient to provide sinful man with a plan for redemption. Yet, Satan has deceived many into believing, "One religion is as good as another." There are thousands of religions. There are also many different versions of Christianity. The different views of religion, telling us who to worship and how to worship, have come about through the deceptive influence of Satan. Satan vehemently fights the truth of Acts 4:12, which says, "Neither is there salvation in any other: for there is none other name under heaven given among men, whereby we must be saved." No other message in the history of man can compare to the message of the gospel. Yet, Satan's deceptive ability has led many to forsake God and place their trust in his lies and reject God's truths.

Satan is not as concerned how one worships on Sunday morning as he is in how one lives during the week. If he can prevent one from living a life of service, prevent one from being thankful for God's goodness and blessings, prevent one from confessing any known sin, prevent one from expecting God to answer prayers, prevent one from loving others as they should, he knows their Sunday morning worship service will not be a meaningful experience. In many churches across America, Satan has progressively removed Christ as the focus of worship and replaced true worship with emotional entertainment. Satan knows what is used in many churches to draw a crowd will not be of eternal benefit to the kingdom of God.

True worship begins with an understanding of "Who" is being worshiped. The focus of worship should not be on the preacher, the minister of music, the choir, the Sunday School class, the building, or one's friendship with fellow church members. True worship is God-centered, not man-centered. If one does not live out his love for God during the week, what they do on Sunday morning has no semblance of true worship.

God is forsaken by False Preachers

As God has His ministers (preachers, evangelist, Bible teachers, church leaders, etc.), Satan also has his false ministers. Paul speaks to this fact in II Corinthians 11:13-15:

> For such are false apostles, deceitful workers, transforming themselves into the apostles of Christ. And no marvel; for Satan himself is transformed into an angel of light. Therefore it is no great thing if his ministers also be transformed as the ministers of righteousness; whose end shall be according to their works.

In that many American's are biblically ignorant of God's Word, it has become an easy task for the false preacher to deceive his congregation. These false preachers wrap themselves in the veneer of kindness, being ever mindful not to offend those who pay their salary. They preach messages that present only the positive side of the gospel. They are afraid to preach the whole gospel. They remain behind the shield of denominational and political correctness. They are cautious not to preach against drinking, abortion, political injustice, and God's requirements for daily living, judgment, or hell. They are careful not to say anything that might offend church members whose lives are in violation of the simplest of God's requirements. God, deliver us from preachers who are afraid to preach against sin. Jeremiah's message from God to the pastors of his day was:

> Woe be unto the pastors that destroy and scatter the sheep of my pasture! saith the LORD. Therefore thus saith the LORD

> God of Israel against the pastors that feed my people; Ye have scattered my flock, and driven them away, and have not visited them: behold, I will visit upon you the evil of your doings, saith the LORD (Jeremiah 23:1-2).

In II Peter 3:3-12, Peter warns, in the last days, Satan will use individuals to influence people to reject God and distrust His Word.

> Knowing this first, that there shall come in the last days scoffers, walking after their own lusts, And saying, Where is the promise of his coming? for since the fathers fell asleep, all things continue as they were from the beginning of the creation. For this they willingly are ignorant of, that by the word of God the heavens were of old, and the earth standing out of the water and in the water: Whereby the world that then was, being overflowed with water, perished: But the heavens and the earth, which are now, by the same word are kept in store, reserved unto fire against the day of judgment and perdition of ungodly men. But, beloved, be not ignorant of this one thing, that one day is with the Lord as a thousand years, and a thousand years as one day. The Lord is not slack concerning his promise, as some men count slackness; but is longsuffering to us-ward, not willing that any should perish, but that all should come to repentance. But the day of the Lord will

come as a thief in the night; in the which the heavens shall pass away with a great noise, and the elements shall melt with fervent heat, the earth also and the works that are therein shall be burned up. Seeing then that all these things shall be dissolved, what manner of persons ought ye to be in all holy conversation and godliness, Looking for and hasting unto the coming of the day of God, wherein the heavens being on fire shall be dissolved, and the elements shall melt with fervent heat? (II Peter 3:3-12).

Americans deny personal sin

Most Americans believe sin exists, but most Americans have a difference of opinion of what constitutes a sin. While some believe drinking is a sin, others do not. Every day in America twenty-eight people, die in automobile accidents related to drivers under the influence of alcohol. The annual cost of alcohol-related automobile accidents exceeds forty-four billion dollars. Alcohol robs employers of countless hours of work each year. Alcohol is a cause of spousal and children abuse causing many to live is constant fear, going without food or proper clothing. Alcohol is linked to more murders in America than any other substance. (79) Many Americans suffer physically because of the amount of alcohol they consume. The wisest of all men, Solomon, said in Proverbs, chapter, 20:1, "Wine is a mocker, strong drink is raging: and whosoever is deceived thereby is not wise."

Some believe abortion is a sin. Yet, others not only perform abortions, they profit from the abortions they conduct. Since the Supreme Court legalized abortion in 1973, upward of sixty million babies have been aborted in

America. Solomon reminds us, in Proverbs 6:17, God hates the shedding of innocent blood. Some, who are in favor of abortion, argue that life does not begin until the baby is out of the womb. Therefore, abortion is neither murder nor a sin. However, if a pregnant mother dies due to the fault of another, her child comes under the Unborn Victims of Violence Act of 2004 (Public Law 108-212). (78) This law recognizes the fetus as a human and the guilty party is charged with a double homicide. Jeremiah tells us in Jeremiah 1:5 that God said of him, "Before I formed thee in the belly I knew thee; and before thou camest forth out of the womb I sanctified thee, and I ordained thee a prophet unto the nations." God saw Jeremiah as a human with great potential while he was in his mother's womb.

Some believe homosexuality is a sin. Some believe people are born homosexual and have no choice in their sexual preference. For many years, sodomy was a felony in America. Yet, in a 6 to 3 decision by the Supreme Court in 2003, the sodomy law was struck down, invalidating sodomy laws making same-sex activity legal in every state and territory. In Romans 1:25-28, the apostle Paul records that God declares homosexuality is a sin.

Sin is not identified by the opinion of the majority. God alone determines what constitutes sin. The Apostle Paul shares, "Know ye not that the unrighteous shall not inherit the kingdom of God? Be not deceived: neither fornicators, nor idolaters, nor adulterers, nor effeminate, nor abusers of themselves with mankind, nor thieves, nor covetous, nor drunkards, nor revilers, nor extortioners, shall inherit the kingdom of God" (1Corinthians 6:9-10). Sin is not only revealed by what one does; sin is also revealed by who one is. Paul, in Romans 3:23, shared with the Church in Rome, "For all have sinned and come short of the glory of God." The Bible defines sin as the breaking, or transgression, of

God's law (1 John 3:4). Sin is also described as disobedience or rebellion against God (Deuteronomy 9:7).

In Jeremiah 2:28, Jeremiah shared with the people of Judah, "As the thief is ashamed when he is found, so is the house of Israel ashamed; they, their kings, their princes, and their priests, and their prophets." The people of America, like the people of Judah are ashamed of their sinful deeds only when they are personally confronted by those sinful deeds. Spiritual callousness occurs when one's heart becomes obstinate toward God. Paul shares, as one refuses to deal with sin over a period of time, they will become spiritually calloused. Paul speaks of this in Ephesians 4:18, "Having the understanding darkened, being alienated from the life of God through the ignorance that is in them, because of the blindness of their heart." The spiritual callousness of America toward God becomes obvious when one considers, as God is being ostracized, American's sit silent.

Sinfulness is akin to the story of the frog who was placed in a pot of water and the pot placed on the stove. As this analogy illustrates, as the water is heating, the frog grows accustomed to the heat of the water. The frog is content until it becomes too late and he realizes the temperature of the water has become unbearable. Americans, like the people of Judah have become progressively acclimated to sin. God will soon judge America.

Chapter 4

PREPARING FOR GOD'S JUDGMENT

Denying the inevitable will not change what will happen. Speaking of the last days, the Bible reveals two major events will occur --- the coming of Christ and the coming of the antichrist. Both of these events are much closer than most think they are.

The Coming of Christ

Permit me to share a few of the reference found in the New Testament concerning the second coming of Christ.

Matthew 25:31-46

> When the Son of man shall come in his glory, and all the holy angels with him, then shall he sit upon the throne of his glory: And before him shall be gathered all nations: and he shall separate them one from another, as a shepherd divideth his sheep from the goats: And he shall set the sheep on his right hand, but the goats on

the left. Then shall the King say unto them on his right hand, Come, ye blessed of my Father, inherit the kingdom prepared for you from the foundation of the world: For I was an hungred, and ye gave me meat: I was thirsty, and ye gave me drink: I was a stranger, and ye took me in: Naked, and ye clothed me: I was sick, and ye visited me: I was in prison, and ye came unto me. Then shall the righteous answer him, saying, Lord, when saw we thee an hungred, and fed thee? or thirsty, and gave thee drink? When saw we thee a stranger, and took thee in? or naked, and clothed thee? Or when saw we thee sick, or in prison, and came unto thee? And the King shall answer and say unto them, Verily I say unto you, Inasmuch as ye have done it unto one of the least of these my brethren, ye have done it unto me. Then shall he say also unto them on the left hand, Depart from me, ye cursed, into everlasting fire, prepared for the devil and his angels: For I was an hungred, and ye gave me no meat: I was thirsty, and ye gave me no drink: I was a stranger, and ye took me not in: naked, and ye clothed me not: sick, and in prison, and ye visited me not. Then shall they also answer him, saying, Lord, when saw we thee an hungred, or athirst, or a stranger, or naked, or sick, or in prison, and did not minister unto thee? Then shall he answer them, saying, Verily I say unto you, Inasmuch as ye did it not to one of the least of these, ye did it not to me. And these shall go away into everlasting punishment: but the righteous into life eternal.

Matthew 24:42-44

Watch therefore: for ye know not what hour your Lord doth come. But know this, that if the goodman of the house had known in what watch the thief would come, he would have watched, and would not have suffered his house to be broken up. Therefore be ye also ready: for in such an hour as ye think not the Son of man cometh.

Acts 17:31

Because he hath appointed a day, in the which he will judge the world in righteousness by that man whom he hath ordained; whereof he hath given assurance unto all men, in that he hath raised him from the dead.

Revelation 20:11-15

And I saw a great white throne, and him that sat on it, from whose face the earth and the heaven fled away; and there was found no place for them. And I saw the dead, small and great, stand before God; and the books were opened: and another book was opened, which is the book of life: and the dead were judged out of those

> things which were written in the books, according to their works. And the sea gave up the dead which were in it; and death and hell delivered up the dead which were in them: and they were judged every man according to their works. And death and hell were cast into the lake of fire. This is the second death. And whosoever was not found written in the book of life was cast into the lake of fire.

Despite the fact, these passages of scripture and many more, both in the Old Testament and in the New Testament, declare the Second Coming of Christ, Peter tells us there will be those in the last days who will scoff at what the Bible says about the coming of Christ, even denying the fact of His coming. In II Peter 3:3-11, Peter says:

> Knowing this first, that there shall come in the last days scoffers, walking after their own lusts, And saying, Where is the promise of his coming? for since the fathers fell asleep, all things continue as they were from the beginning of the creation. For this they willingly are ignorant of, that by the word of God the heavens were of old, and the earth standing out of the water and in the water: Whereby the world that then was, being overflowed with water, perished: But the heavens and the earth, which are now, by the same word are kept in store, reserved unto fire against the day of judgment and perdition of ungodly men. But, beloved, be not ignorant of this one thing,

> that one day is with the Lord as a thousand years, and a thousand years as one day. The Lord is not slack concerning his promise, as some men count slackness; but is longsuffering to us-ward, not willing that any should perish, but that all should come to repentance. But the day of the Lord will come as a thief in the night; in the which the heavens shall pass away with a great noise, and the elements shall melt with fervent heat, the earth also and the works that are therein shall be burned up. Seeing then that all these things shall be dissolved, what manner of persons ought ye to be in all holy conversation and godliness,

Jeremiah challenged his people to "look and see." Pause for a moment and consider what the Bible says of the condition of the world and the church, prior to the coming of Christ. We are hearing of wars and rumors of wars. Earthquakes are becoming common events. We are hearing more and more about worldwide sickness, and famines, and strange events occurring in the atmosphere. The church is undergoing a decline (II Thessalonians 2:3). Many are departing from the faith and embracing demonic spirits (I Timothy 4:1). Things are bad, but the Bible tells us the spiritual condition of the world will become worse as we approach the coming of Christ.

Jesus tells us, in Mark 13:22, in the last days, "...false Christ and false prophets shall rise, and shall shew signs and wonders, to seduce, if it were possible even the elect." Despite the clear and present danger occurring today, Peter warns the scoffer of God's patience and reminds them not to be ignorant of the fact of God's promise to come as a thief in the night with severe judgment. The question that demands an answer is, "How should you be living to be prepared for what the future holds?"

Politically, spiritually, morally and socially, America is sick. Our news media has become an agent for the progressive's and socialist's propaganda. Americans are learning of the deep corruption affecting many of our nation's political leaders. Members of our most trusted institutions have sought to betray our Constitutional right to an honest election for the office of the President. Governors and city officials of sanctuary states and cities, defy federal law with impunity, while the average citizen would be arrested, tried, and jailed, for defying federal law.

As these events occur, there is no outcry against them from most pulpits across America. Messages that reveal the deplorable, spiritual condition of America and the church are not palatable. Such messages sadden people. Many pastors have concluded they had rather please their people than share God's truth. However, these pastors will give an account to God for their lack of conviction and courage to share God's truth. Jeremiah was more concerned about God's truth than he was in what those around him thought. He did not pattern his life, or alter his message, to be like some "big preacher" who was considered popular. He was content to please God. He was willing to suffer for the sake of the truth.

Paul reminds us in 2 Timothy 4:3-4, "For the time will come when they will not endure sound doctrine, but after their own lusts shall they heap to themselves teachers, having itching ears; And they shall turn away their ears from the truth, and shall be turned unto fables." Knowing that the coming of Christ will be as a "thief in the night" and He could come at any moment, we need to be ready (I Thessalonians 5:2). We need to be standing firm on God's

Word and following His principles and promises. We need to be telling others about Christ and encouraging them to be ready for his return.

The coming of the antichrist

After the Coming of Christ and the Rapture of the church, the False Prophet and the Antichrist will come on the World's stage. At the Second Coming of Christ, Christians will be raptured out of the world, but will see and experience a foretaste of what will occur during the Tribulation period. Ezekiel 28 tells us Satan, before his fall, was an angel of the highest rank and a leader of worship in heaven. Isaiah 14 tells us, Satan's fall had to do with his desire to be equal to or greater than God, John, in Revelation 12:7-10 speaks of Satan's fall. John says:

> And there was war in heaven: Michael and his angels fought against the dragon; and the dragon fought and his angels, And prevailed not; neither was their place found any more in heaven. And the great dragon was cast out, that old serpent, called the Devil, and Satan, which deceiveth the whole world: he was cast out into the earth, and his angels were cast out with him. And I heard a loud voice saying in heaven, Now is come salvation, and strength, and the kingdom of our God, and the power of his Christ: for the accuser of our brethren is cast down, which accused them before our God day and night.

The first recorded appearance of Satan after being cast out of heaven was to Eve in the Garden of Eden, as a serpent. Satan believed if he could deceive Adam and Eva, cause them to sin, he would defeat God's plan for humanity. God was not caught off guard by Satan's actions, nor by Adam or Eve's disobedience. In Genesis 3:15, God informed Eve through her seed a child would be born who would defeat Satan. This child to be born was the promise of the Messiah.

Throughout the Old Testament Satan's attempts to prevent the birth of Christ are evident. According to the apostle John, after Christ was born, Satan sent a spirit of antichrist into the world, denying that Christ was born in the flesh. John speaks of a spirit that opposed the teaching that Christ lived in a human body. In I John 4:3, John says, "And every spirit that confesseth not that Jesus Christ is come in the flesh is not of God: and this is that spirit of antichrist, whereof ye have heard that it should come; and even now already is it in the world." In II John 2:7, John says, "For many deceivers are entered into the world, who confess not that Jesus Christ is come in the flesh. This is a deceiver and an antichrist." End-time prophecies show that religious people, including professing Christians, can be deceived into accepting a counterfeit Christianity and will oppose many of the teachings of Christ. This spirit of antichrist is not the antichrist that will appear in the last days. The antichrist is yet to come.

The Antichrist and the False Prophet

Satan is preparing the world for the ultimate deception that will finalize in the coming of the Antichrist and the false Prophet. Who are these two individuals? When will they be revealed? How will they be identified? These and many other questions are often asked about the False

Prophet and the Antichrist. Paul tells us in II Thessalonians 2:4, Satan continues his objective to overthrow God. Paul says of Satan, "Who opposes and exalts himself above all that is called God, or that is worshipped, so that he sits as God in the temple of God, showing himself that he is God."

When God raptures the Church from the world and the Spirit of God no longer stands in opposition to the world's sin, there will be a spiritual, moral, social, economic, political crises that will occur that will be so bad, the mind of man cannot comprehend. It will be in this environment, the people of the world will cry out for a world leader to resolve the world's problems. The condition of the world is growing worse day by day. The population of the world is already growing restless and clamoring for answers to the world's problems.

The False Prophet, like the Antichrist, will be a mortal who is demon possessed. He will be a religious leader, in all probability a professing Christian. His appearance will be Christ-like, but his message will be demonic. He will have the ability to cause the majority of the world's population to worship the Antichrist. He will do this by exalting the Antichrist through his oratorical abilities and by the deceptive miracles that he performs. He will also exercise judicial powers, forcing individuals to worship the Antichrist through a mandated purchasing system that requires individuals to have a branded number placed on their right hand or on their forehead before they can buy or sell.

The stage for the False Prophet is being set today by false preachers and especially by those whose ministry is established on faith healing. Even today, crowds of thousands gather to observe the performances of preachers who claim to have the gift of healing from God. How close are we to the coming of the Antichrist? The condition of the world politically, morally, spiritually, and militarily indicates we must be close. In every facet of life, Satan's influence is prominent. Never has the world or the church been more out of tune with God and His purpose for humanity, than today. Leaders in our own government have been sharing their plea for a "One World Government." Most often, they mask their request by identifying themselves as "Globalist." President Obama and other America Presidents have advocated that America should be a submissive partner to the globalist agenda. President Trump's stance against globalism is providing a momentary reprieve from the coming of the Antichrist. This is only a reprieve; he will come.

The attacks against gun ownership by liberals in America, if effected, will assist in the effort to bring about globalism. (79) It is only when Americans are unable to defend themselves that the government will be able to force their globalist agenda on the American people. Consider the following:

- In 1911: Turkey established gun control. From 1915-1917, 1.5 million Christian Armenians were murdered.
- In 1929: The Soviet Union established gun control. From 1929-1953, 20 million dissidents were murdered.
- In 1935: China established gun control. From 1948-1952, 20 million political dissidents were murdered.
- In 1938: Germany established gun control. From 1939-1945 13 million Jews and others were murdered.
- In 1956: Cambodia established gun control. From 1975-1977, 1 million people were murdered.
- In 1964: Guatemala established gun control. From 1981-1984, 100,000 Mayan Indians were murdered

- In 1970: Uganda established gun control. From 1971-1979, 300,000 Christians were murdered.
- More than 56 million defenseless people, in the twentieth century were murdered by governments implementing gun control.

Before the return of the Lord, there will be a time when many will turn their backs on the Lord. The Apostle Paul teaches, "Now the Spirit speaketh expressly, that in the latter times some shall depart from the faith, giving heed to seducing spirits, and doctrines of devils; Speaking lies in hypocrisy; having their conscience seared with a hot iron" (I Timothy 4:1-2). Matthew tells us just prior to the coming of Christ will be marked by sexual perversion. He says, "And because iniquity shall abound, the love of many shall wax cold" (Matthew 24:12). Jesus said, just prior to His return, will be a time of great violence. It will be a time on earth as it was during the days of Noah (Matthew 24:37). Concerning the days of Noah, Moses says, "The Lord saw that the wickedness of man was great in the earth, and that every intention of the thoughts of his heart was only evil continually" (Genesis 6:5). Each of these events reveals the time just prior to the coming of Christ will be extremely evil. We are living in the beginning of this period. Things are bad, but the worst is yet to come.

As previously noted, to know what God is doing, observe the nation of Israel. The nations surrounding Israel desire Israel's destruction. Ezekiel 12 reveals that, prior to the coming of Christ, Israel will become a place of contention for the whole world. Recently, only seven of the 193 United Nation States voted with America to recognize Jerusalem as the capital of Israel. From all indications, we are on the verge of the Coming of Christ.

The Bible tells us, during this period, the Antichrist, the greatest political leader the world has ever known, will be introduced and come to power out of one of the European countries (Daniel 11). This event will occur shortly after the Rapture of the Church. When the antichrist assumes his position as the world's leader, he will orchestrate a peace treaty with Israel and her enemies. Israel and the world will acclaim his greatness. The rule of the antichrist will last for seven years and will be divided into two periods. As bad as the evil events in the world will become during the Tribulation period, these evils will pale in comparison to the evil that will occur during the Great Tribulation period. Some believe Isaiah 28:14-18 refers to this treaty:

> Wherefore hear the word of the LORD, ye scornful men that rule this people, which is in Jerusalem. Because ye have said, We have made a covenant with death, and with hell are we at agreement; when the overflowing scourge shall pass through, it shall not come unto us: for we have made lies our refuge, and under falsehood have we hid ourselves: Therefore thus saith the Lord GOD, Behold, I lay in Zion for a foundation a stone, a tried stone, a precious corner stone, a sure foundation: he that believeth shall not make haste. Judgment also will I lay to the line, and righteousness to the plummet: and the hail shall sweep away the refuge of lies, and the waters shall overflow the hiding place. And your covenant with death shall be disannulled, and your agreement with hell shall not stand; when the

overflowing scourge shall pass through, then ye shall be trodden down by it.

Dangerous times are coming

The Bible presents clear and unequivocal evidence that before Christ returns the world will digress into a spiritual quagmire. Matthew tells us, "The love of many will grow cold." (Matthew 24:12). II Thessalonians 2:3 says "Let no man deceive you by any means: for that day shall not come, except there come a falling away first, and that man of sin be revealed, the son of perdition." Paul says, in II Timothy 3:1-5:

> This know also, that in the last days perilous times shall come. For men shall be lovers of their own selves, covetous, boasters, proud, blasphemers, disobedient to parents, unthankful, unholy, Without natural affection, trucebreakers, false accusers, incontinent, fierce, despisers of those that are good, Traitors, heady, highminded, lovers of pleasures more than lovers of God; Having a form of godliness, but denying the power thereof: from such turn away.

Over twenty years ago, I began preaching a message across America entitled, "Has America Gone Too Far?" Many have asked me to put this message into a book and make it available that all Americans could have an opportunity to hear its truths. I can honestly say, writing this book has been the most difficult undertaking of my life. I have been studying, gathering information, writing, and rewriting this book for more than eight years. I have placed the writing of this book on the back shelf on several occasions, spending months in prayer and wondering if I am doing God's will. I have a personal understanding with Jeremiah, the weeping prophet, of how sharing the judgment of God upon the nation you love can crush your spirit. I have a kinship with Jeremiah's brokenness in that God informed him his nation would not accept his message, nor would they repent and return to God. I can also say with Jeremiah, "There is a fire in my bones and I must share what I believe God has given me to share." The question that has caused me the most grief, and I am sure it was the same with Jeremiah, is "How can I do a better job of telling people what they must do to prepare for God's judgment?"

What should the non-Christian do?

The non-Christian is at a serious disadvantage concerning spiritual matters. They are not involved in church, and most non-Christians have little or no interest in studying the Bible. They are unfamiliar with God's Word that teaches, "I also will choose their delusions, and will bring their fears upon them; because when I called, none did answer; when I spake, they did not hear: but they did evil before mine eyes, and chose that in which I delighted not" (Isaiah 66:4). Nor do they embrace the truth of, Jeremiah 6:19 that says, "Hear, O earth: behold, I will bring evil upon this people, even the fruit of their thoughts, because they have not hearkened unto my words, nor to my law, but rejected it."

The author of Hebrews warns the non-Christian of God's judgment, "See that ye refuse not him that speaketh. For if they escaped not who refused him that spake on earth, much more shall not we escape, if we turn away from him that speaketh from heaven" (Hebrews 12:25). Though the non-Christian may not know what God has in store for America's sinfulness, ignorance of the truth is no excuse. Isaiah 13:11 says, "Thus I will punish the world for its evil, and the wicked for their iniquity; and I will cause the arrogance of the proud to cease, and will lay low the haughtiness of the terrible."

For forty years, Jeremiah preached God would judge Judah. He was hated, ridiculed, beaten, imprisoned; some even sought to kill him. The people of Judah refused to believe they were sinful, though the evidence of their sinfulness was evident. They placed their hope in God's protection and provision for them on experiences. They remembered when the Assyrian Army encamped around Jerusalem with 185,000 troops (II Kings 19:35). They remembered how God sent an angel and destroyed the 185,000 Assyrian troops in one night. They remembered the stories handed down from their parents and grandparents of how God had delivered their ancestors from Egypt and gave them victory after victory over their enemies, as God brought them into the Promise Land. They believed they were God's chosen people; He would never permit another nation to carry them from Judah into captivity. They were comforted by the messages of the false priest and prophets who shared with them messages of peace, protection, and prosperity. As time passed, they became calloused. God's loving kindness and tender mercies eventually reached the end of God's patience and God declared them incurable, (II Chronicles 36:16). God's judgment became a reality.

Jeremiah's account of Judah's sinfulness and their disbelief that God would judge them is a clear description of America today. Americans, as the people of Judah, are of the opinion God has provided for, and protected, America in the past. He will continue to do so. America, like Judah, has spiritual leaders that are convinced God loves America too much to judge America. One must ask, "If God judged Judah for the same sins America is committing --- will God refrain from judging America?"

Before God extends His judgment, He "woos" and warns." God's love for the people of Judah, through the messages of Jeremiah, was clearly illustrated. God commissioned Jeremiah before he was born to take a message to the nations, and specifically to Judah, urging a change of heart. Despite the sinfulness of the people of Judah, God loved them, and extended to them His forgiving grace. God has done no less for America. Despite America's forsaking God, as evidenced by the decline of the church, the removal of God and prayer form our schools, the murdering of millions of unborn children, the corruption of political and spiritual leaders, and people embracing and supporting social issues the Bible clearly condemns, God has faithfully wooed Americans to repent and return to Him.

The thought of non-Christians being unprepared for what America is going through, and the ultimate judgment of God upon America that will soon occur, should cause the members of the church to be more spiritually concerned for the lost. When thousands of America's churches have not baptized anyone in years; when revivals are no longer considered; when training for church members to be effective witnesses is no longer important, it can be said, "That church has lost its first love."

Every year 4,000 churches close their doors permanently in America. Thirty-five-hundred church members are leaving the church every day, resulting in 1,277,000 leaving the church in America every year. There are approximately 250,000 Protestant churches in America. It is estimated that 200,000 of these church, or 80% of them, have either leveled off their growth, or they are in decline. (80) These statistics should be frightening to both the Christian and the non-Christian. Paul asked, in Romans 10:14, "How then shall they call on him in whom they have not believed? and how shall they believe in him of whom they have not heard? and how shall they hear without a preacher?" If the members of the church do not share with the lost, they will never know nor be prepared for what the future holds. The only hope for the non-Christian is a personal relationship with Christ.

What should the Christian do?

John's message in the Book of Revelation is two-fold: the judgment of God and the ultimate victory of the redeemed. To each of the seven churches of Asia, John records that God said He knew their works, and then John shares with them God's rebuke. John informs his readers, before Christ returns and Christians experience the victory God has promised, God will judge His church. God's judgment of the church will affect those within the church and those of whom the church is responsible for reaching with the truth of God's Word. If each of the seven churches in the book of Revelation represents a period for the church, we are living in the Laodicea Age, or the last days of the church. The church of Laodicea is described in Revelation 3:14-22:

> And unto the angel of the church of the Laodiceas write; These things saith the Amen, the faithful and true witness, the beginning of the creation of God; I know thy works, that thou art neither cold nor hot: I would thou wert cold or hot. So then because thou art lukewarm, and neither cold nor hot, I will spue thee out of my mouth. Because thou sayest, I am rich,

and increased with goods, and have need of nothing; and knowest not that thou art wretched, and miserable, and poor, and blind, and naked: I counsel thee to buy of me gold tried in the fire, that thou mayest be rich; and white raiment, that thou mayest be clothed, and that the shame of thy nakedness do not appear; and anoint thine eyes with eyesalve, that thou mayest see. As many as I love, I rebuke and chasten: be zealous therefore, and repent. Behold, I stand at the door, and knock: if any man hear my voice, and open the door, I will come in to him, and will sup with him, and he with me. To him that overcometh will I grant to sit with me in my throne, even as I also overcame, and am set down with my Father in his throne. He that hath an ear, let him hear what the Spirit saith unto the churches.

The church of today, is like the church of Laodicea. It is so spiritually depraved; it cannot recognize it's on spiritual depravity. John said the church at Laodicea made God sick. Most churches today are spiritually depraved, having little or no spiritual impact on their community. Peter reminds us in I Peter 4:17, "For the time is come that judgment must begin at the house of God: and if it first begin at us, what shall the end be of them that obey not the gospel of God?" Evidence would indicate God is already withdrawing His Spirit from many churches.

When Paul wrote his epistle to the church at Corinth, he revealed there were three groups of people that comprised the church's membership (I Corinthians 2:14-3:3) --- the lost, the saved, and the carnal.

> But the natural man receiveth not the things of the Spirit of God: for they are foolishness unto him: neither can he know them, because they are spiritually discerned. But he that is spiritual judgeth all things, yet he himself is judged of no man. For who hath known the mind of the Lord, that he may instruct him? but we have the mind of Christ. And I, brethren, could not speak unto you as unto spiritual, but as unto carnal, even as unto babes in Christ. I have fed you with milk, and not with meat: for hitherto ye were not able to bear it, neither yet now are ye able. For ye are yet carnal: for whereas there is among you envying, and strife, and divisions, are ye not carnal, and walk as men?

If you profess to know Christ as your Savior, the first thing you should do to prepare for God's judgment on America is to make sure of your relationship with Christ (II Corinthians 13:5).

Everyone who professes to be a Christian should examine his or her relationship with Christ. According to Southern Baptist statistics, only 3 to 5 percent of church members tithe, only 3 percent ever win another person to Christ and only 12 percent do the ministry of the church. These statistics reveal that many in the church are either lost or carnal. Helping others to be prepared for God's judgment on America requires one to be spiritually right with God themselves. When the people of Judah refused to believe they had forsaken God, Jeremiah asked them to "look and see." If you looked back over your life, could you honestly say, "I know Christ as my Savior and my daily living demonstrates this as a fact?" Could you say this?

Every Christian should be involved in a Bible believing church and do all they can to win as many as possible to Christ. In Matthew 16:18, Jesus said, "I will build my church." The church is the only institution Jesus said He would build. He builds His church through His followers. In Ephesians 4:11-16, we are told how the church is organized and what each member is to do.

> And He Himself gave some *to be* apostles, some prophets, some evangelists, and some pastors and teachers, for the equipping of the saints for the work of ministry, for the edifying of the body of Christ, till we all come to the unity of the faith and of the knowledge of the Son of God, to a perfect man, to the measure of the stature of the fullness of Christ; that we should no longer be children, tossed to and fro and carried about with every wind of doctrine, by the trickery of men, in the cunning craftiness of deceitful plotting, but, speaking the truth in love, may grow up in all things into Him who is the head—Christ—from whom the whole body, joined and knit together by what every joint supplies, according to the effective working by which every part does its share, causes growth of the body for the edifying of itself in love.

Note what these verses teach concerning God's design for the building of His Church.

1. He has provided the church with leaders, Apostles, Prophets, Evangelists, and Pastor/Teachers.
2. He has assigned these leaders the responsibility of equipping the saints (Christians) for the work of the church.
3. He has assigned these leaders with the responsibility of educating the saints in the Word of God that they may grow in their faith and become spiritually mature.
4. The saint should become so anchored in their faith they will not be deceived by false doctrine or tricked by man or Satan into believing anything but God's truth.
5. When sharing the truth of God's word with others, the saint should speak the truth in love.
6. The life of the saint should demonstrate Christlikeness in every area of their life.
7. The saint should join with other saints and work together to glorify Christ.

As a Christian, you have the responsibility of sharing the truth of God's Word with others. Matthew 5:15-16 says, "Neither do men light a candle, and put it under a bushel, but on a candlestick; and it giveth light unto all that are in the house. Let your light so shine before men, that they may see your good works, and glorify your Father which is in heaven."

What is the proof God will Judge America?

The proof God will judge America is found in the trustworthiness of God. Moses tells us in Numbers 23:19, "God is not a man, that he should lie; neither the son of man, that he should repent: hath he said, and shall he not do it? or hath he spoken, and shall he not make it good." The Bible and history show that God will destroy sinful nations that forsake him. Psalm 9:17 says, "The wicked shall be turned into hell, and all the nations that forget God." The people of Judah were well aware of God's judgment upon sinful nations. Yet, they refused to believe God would judge them. This is the prevailing sentiment of most Americans today.

When Will God Judge America?

While Judah was living under the control of the Egyptians and the Babylonians, they remained so foolish as to believe God would not judge them. As long as they were permitted to go about their day-to-day life, they were confident that God would never permit the Egyptians or the Babylonians to remove them from the land God had given them.

Consider what Jeremiah shared with his people in Jeremiah 5:23-29:

> But this people hath a revolting and a rebellious heart; they are revolted and gone. Neither say they in their heart, Let us now fear the LORD our God, that giveth rain, both the former and the latter, in his season: he reserveth unto us the appointed weeks of the harvest. Your iniquities have turned away these things, and your sins

> have withholden good things from you. For among my people are found wicked men: they lay wait, as he that setteth snares; they set a trap, they catch men. As a cage is full of birds, so are their houses full of deceit: therefore they are become great, and waxen rich. They are waxen fat, they shine: yea, they overpass the deeds of the wicked: they judge not the cause, the cause of the fatherless, yet they prosper; and the right of the needy do they not judge. Shall I not visit for these things? saith the LORD: shall not my soul be avenged on such a nation as this?

Most Americans do not believe God will judge their nation. However, considering all the devastating events America has undergone during the past few years, it would appear God's judgment on America has already begun. Consider the following:

Hurricanes

This is a list of hurricanes that made landfall in America over the past twenty-five years. Andrew, Emily, Erin. Opal, Bertha, Fran, Danny, Bonnie, Earl, Georges, Bret, Floyd, Irene, Lili, Claudette, Isabel, Alex, Charley, Gaston, Frances, Ivan, Jeanne, Cindy, Dennis, Katrina, Rita, Wilma, Humberto, Dolly, Gustav, Ike, Irene, Isaac, Sandy, Arthur, Hermine and Matthew, not counting 2017.

Three category 4 hurricanes made landfall in America in 2017, Harvey, Irma, Maria. This was the first time in history that three category 4 hurricanes made landfall in America in one season. Hurricane Harvey made landfall in Texas in

August of 2017 as a category 4 hurricane, causing upward of $180 billion dollars in damages and affected millions of people, leaving more than eighty dead.

On September 10, 2017, Hurricane Irma made landfall in Florida as a category 4 hurricane. It made its way north into Georgia and the Carolinas as a tropical storm leaving over $100 billion dollars in damages in its path and 75 dead. Seven million were forced to evacuate their homes. Hurricane Irma affected every major city in Florida.

On September 20 of 2017, Hurricane Maria hit Puerto Rico, a Territory of the United States, as a category 4 hurricane. Maria was the strongest hurricane to hit Puerto Rico in 85 years with upward of $100 billion dollars in damages. As Maria left Puerto Rico, as a tropical storm it skirted parts of the Eastern coast causing beach erosion. Also in 2017, Nate, a smaller hurricane, made landfall in Mississippi as a category 1 hurricane and effected people in Louisiana, Mississippi, and Alabama with serious flooding. Hurricane Nate caused in excess of one billion dollars in damages.

Tornados

America leads the world with tornados. During a 36-hour period between November 21 and November 23, 1992, a rash of tornados affected 13 states. These tornados started in Houston, Texas and moved across 12 other states. Forty-one of these tornadoes were rated as an F3, and six were rated as an F4. These tornadoes left 26 dead, 638 injured and billions of dollars in damages.

One of the most powerful tornados ever recorded struck Oklahoma in May of 2005 with winds clocked at 340 miles per hour. During April 27-30, 2011, Southerners experienced one of the deadliest tornado outbreaks in American history. More than 340 people died from 15 tornadoes that moved across seven states, including 238 deaths in Alabama. The National Weather Service rated one of these tornados as an EF5, the highest rating given to a tornado. Over 8,000 buildings were destroyed.

There were 1,511 reports of tornadoes in the United States in 2017 of which at least 1,359 were confirmed, leaving billions of dollars in damages. Tornadoes and severe thunderstorms cause as much annual property damage in America as do hurricanes and often cause more deaths.

Drugs

Alcohol is a drug that is classified as a depressant and is the most used drug in America. The CDC reported excessive drinking led to approximately 88,000 deaths in America between 2006 and 2010. (81) The CDC stated alcohol abuse cost America $249 billion dollars in 2010.

After alcohol, marijuana is the drug most addictive. The National Center for Health Statistics revealed there were more than 600,000 drug related deaths in America between 2000 and 2016. This would compute 15 deaths per day. On December 19, 2016, the U.S. Surgeon General reported drug and alcohol misuse cost the American taxpayer more than $440 billion dollars annually.

Wild Fires

During 2011 in Texas, 31,453 fires burned approximately 4,000,000 acres, destroyed 2,947 homes, and over 2,700 other structures. The fires were contributed to a drought that had covered the state for the past three years, and worsened by strong winds, warm temperatures, and low humidity. Timber lost to drought and wildfire in 2011 in Texas could have produced $1.6 billion worth of products, resulting in a 3.4 billion economic impact in East Texas alone.

In 2017, California saw 9,054 wildfires that burnt more than 1,300,000 acres. These fires did more than 180 billion dollars in damage and left forty-six dead. It is estimated that wildfires across America in 2017 destroyed approximately ten million acres at a cost of billions of dollars in damages. As this book is being written, (2018), California is experiencing multiple wild fires. Thousands of structures have burned and many have lost their life. The Mendocino Complex fires have already burned 331,399 acres.

Terror Attacks

In the early sixties, as a sailor aboard the U.S.S. Alamo, in San Diego, California, I was instructed to take a rifle and stand watch on the after part of the ship, with orders to shoot anyone I saw in the water. I was later informed there were terroristic threats made against ships in the harbor of San Diego and against Hoover Dam. During the presidency of Jimmy Carter, I was invited to Washington D.C. to a National Affairs Seminar. We were told terroristic threats were being made against the United States. (82) We were also told that these threats were not told to the American people for fear of creating panic.

Today, when terrorist attacks are discussed, most Americans think of 9/11. On September 11, 2001, nineteen Islamic extremist hijacked four airplanes and carried out suicide attacks against targets in the United States. Two of the planes were flown into the twin towers of the World Trade Center in New York City, a third plane hit the Pentagon just outside Washington, D.C., and the fourth plane was forced to crashed in a field in Pennsylvania. These attacks took the lives of almost three thousand people

On December 2, 2015, a Muslim couple, Syed Farook and Tashfeen Malik, shot, and killed 14 people in San Bernardino, California. (83) On June 12, 2016, Omar Mateen attacked an Orlando gay nightclub, killing fifty people.(84) Mateen later pledged his allegiance to ISIS on a 911 call he made to brag about his actions. This was one of the worst mass shootings in U.S. history. On November 28, 2016, Abdul Razak Ali Artan, an Ohio State University student, ran his car into a group of students and slashed people with a butcher knife. (85) On October 31, 2017, Sayfullo Saipov, from Uzbekistan, drove a rented truck into a crowd of pedestrians and cyclists on a bike path near the World Trade Center in Manhattan. (86) The attack killed eight people and injured at least twelve more. Under the Obama Administration, members of his administration forbade the phrase "Islamic Terrorist." It is believed by many, there are secret terrorist groups stationed across America waiting for the right time to create destruction against America.

Gangs

The Federal Bureau of Investigation website in 2014, estimated there were 33,000 violent street gangs, motorcycle gangs, and prison gangs with approximately 1.4 million members that are criminally active in the United States and Puerto Rico. (87) These gangs are responsible for eighty percent of all crimes in America. The National Gang Center estimates that gangs cost Americans as much as $655 billion dollars annually. A report from the Major Cities Chiefs Association stated, on January 30, violent crime increased in many of the nation's largest cities in 2016, the second year in a row that metro areas saw jumps in homicide, robbery and aggravated assault. (88)

Unknown Events

Satan is a master of deception. As bad as what we can see and know that is occurring around us, what should frighten us most are those things happening privately without being known, or seen by the public? If America knew what was taking place in the shadows, there would be panic in the streets. Satan operates best from the shadows. How many Islamic cell groups are there across America waiting for the right moment to bring about destruction on America? Is there an attempt by some to overthrow our government and establish an America that is totally opposite of what America is today? What is the purpose of America's Educational system for destroying the history of America? I am persuaded many are content not knowing what lurks in the shadows.

Many are asking, "What will it take for God to get America's attention?" Despite the social, political, moral, and spiritual condition of America, the church is in decline. The message from pulpits would have congregations to believe America is on the verge of revival. Messages on the doctrine of the coming of Christ, the judgment of God and the consequences of sinful living are seldom heard. The failure to preach the "whole counsel of God" has led many to believe the social issues God condemns should not be addressed from the pulpit.

In Ezekiel 14, Ezekiel reveals God will orchestrate the events of the last days. God will use ordinary people, political leaders, even allowing Satan to have a part. However, God will be the force behind what will take place. Ezekiel records God as saying, in Ezekiel 14:2, "I will make," in verse 3, "I will strike" in verse 4, "I will open," in verse 6, "I will make," in verse 9, "I will set," in verse 10, "I will pour." Whatever is to take place, God will be the ultimate force that brings it to pass. The question that demands an answer is, "Are you spiritually ready for the judgment God will bring upon America?" If not, why not? What are you willing to do to be prepared for the judgment God will soon bring upon America?

Endnotes

Chapter One

1. Davis, F. (2009), Ae We Really No Longer a Christian Nation? *Market Faith,* Retrieved from http:// marketfaith.org/implications-of-worldview/are-we-really-no-longer-a-christian-nation/
2. Ertelt, S. (2016). 58,586,256 Abortions in America Since Roe v. Wade in 1973. *LifeNe Richest.* Retrieved from https://www.therichest.com/rich-list/10-corrupt-politicians-and-their-prison-sentences/ *ws.* Retrieved from https://www. Lifenews.com/2016/01/14/58586256-abortions-in-america-since-roe-v-wade-in-1973/
3. Duke Cunningham Corruption. (2005), *The San Diego Union-Tribune.* Retrieved from http://centennial.journalism.columbia.edu/wp-content/uploads.2013/03/76, Duke-Cunningham-and-Corruption-pdf
4. Gary, M. & Snyder, S. J. (2011), Sinful Statement Larry Craig, *Time.* Retrieved from http://content.time.com/time/specials/2007/article/0,28804,1721111_1721210_1721118,00.html
5. Hamilton L. (2014). 10 Corrupt Politicians and Their Prison Sentences. *The*

6. Erb, K.P. (2016), IRS Targeting Scandal: Citizens United, Lois Lerner And the $20M Tax Saga That Won't Go Away. *Forbes.* Retrieved from https://www.forbes.com/sites/kellphillipserb/2016/06/24/irs-targeting-scandal-citizens-united-lois-lerner-and-the-20m-tax-saga-that-wont-go-away/#78541131bed1
7. Sekulow, J. (201). Lois Lerner got off easy in the IRS scandal. It's time to reexamine the targeting of conservatives. *Fox News Network, LLC.* Retrieved from https://www.foxnews.com/opinion/lois-lerner-got-off-easy-in-the-irs-scandal-its-time-to-reexamine-the-targeting-of-conservatives.
8. Rein L. & Davidson, J. (2012). GSA chief resigns amid reports of excessive spending, *The Washington Post.* Retrieved from htts://www.washingtonpost.com/politics/gsa-chief-resigns-amid-reports-of-excessive-spending/2012/04/02/glQABLNNrS_story.html?noredirect=on&utm_term=.0604cabo422d
9. Benghazi Terrorist Attact. (2013), Retrieved from https://youtube.com/watch timecontinue=193&v=QSooz2wXpes
10. Alvarez, P. (2016). What Happened the Night of the Benghazi Attack? *The Atlantic.* Retrieved from https:/www.theatlantic.com/politics/archive/2016/house-republicans-benghazi-report-hillary-clinton/489125/
11. Carnevale, M. L. (2009): If you Like Your Doctor, You Can Keep Your Doctor'. *The Wall Street Journal.* Retrieved from https://blogs.wsj.com/com/washwire/2009/06/15/obama-if-you-like-your-doctor-you-can-keep-your-doctor/
12. Krauthammer, C. (2014). The Gruber Confession. *The Washington Post.* Retrieved from https://www.washingtonpost.com/

opinions/charles-krauthammer-the-gruber-confession/2014/11/13/474595bc-6b6b-11e4-9fb4-a622dae742a2_story.html?noredirect=on&utm_term=.3eb2d050a703

13. Landler, M. & Lichibian, E. (2016). F.B.I. Director James Comey Recommends No Charges for Hillary Clinton on Email. *New York Times.* Retrieved from https://www.nytimes.com/2016/07/06/us/politics/hillary-clinton-fbi-email-comey.html

14. Casebeer, G. A. (2016). Comey Has a Long History of Letting The Clintons Off The Hook. *The Bern Report.* Retrieved from http://the bernreport.com/comey-long-history-letting-clintons-off-hook/

15. Landler, M. & Lichtblau, E. (2016). F.B.I. Director James Comey Recommends No Charges for Hillary Clinton on Email. *New York Times.* Retrieved from https://www.nytimes.com/2016/07/06/us/politics/hillary-clinton-fbi-email-comey.html

16. McCarthy, A. C. (2017). The Obama Administration's Uranium One Scandal. *National Review.* Retrieved from https://www.nationalreview.com/2017/10/uranium-one-deal-obama-administration-doj-hillary-clinton-racketeering/

17. Huston, W. T. (2011). The Top 50 Liberal Media Bias Examples. *Western Journal.* Retrieved from https://www.westernjournal.com/top-50-examples-liberal-media-bias/

18. Huff, E. (2018). Glenn Greenwald warns: MSNBC a deep state propaganda extension of the corrupt CIA. Natural News. Retrieved from https://www.naturalnews.com/2018-07-10-glenn-greenwald-warns-msnbc-a-deep-state-propaganda-extension-of-the-corrupt-cia.html

19. Becker, J. & McIntire, M. (2015). Cash Flowed to Clinton Foundation Amid Russian Uranium Deal. *The New York Times.* Retrieved from https://www.nytimes.com/2015/04/24/us/cash-flowed-to-clinton-foundation-as-russians-pressed-for-control-of-uranium-company.html
20. Gregory, P. R. (2017). The Trump Dossier Is Fake And Here Are The Reasons Why. *Forbes.* Retrieved from ttps://www.forbes.com/sites/paulroderickgregory/2017/01/13/the-trump-dossier-is-false-news-and-heres-why/#54966f856867
21. Berman, M. (2014). Here is everything police and witnesses said happened when Michael Brown was killed. *The Washington Post.* Retrieved from https://www.washingtonpost.com/news/post-nation/wp/2014/08/21/here-is-everything-police-and-witnesses-said-happened-when-michael-brown-was-killed/?utm_term=.038ac707aee4
22. Flurry, G. (2016). The Real Agenda Behind Black Lives Matter. *The Trumpet.* Retrieved from https://www.thetrumpet.com/13722-the-real-agenda-behind-black-lives-matter
23. Hoft, J. (2016). UNREAL. Obama Invites Radical #BlackLivesMatter Leader to White House After His Arrest Last Weekend. *The Gateway Pundit.* Retrieved from https://www.thegatewaypundit.com/2016/07/obama-invites-radical-blacklivesmatter-leader-white-house-arrest-last-weekend/
24. Mindock, C. (2018). Taking a knee: Why are NFL players protesting and when did they start to kneel? *Independent.* Retrieved from https://www.independent.co.uk/news/world/americas/us-politics/taking-a-knee-national-anthem-nfl-trump-why-meaning-origins-racism-us-colin-kaepernick-a8521741.html

25. Resendes. (2002). Church allowed abuse by priest for years. *Boston Globe.* Retrieved from https://www.bostonglobe.com/news/special-reports/2002/01/06/church-allowed-abuse-priest-for-years/cSHfGkTIrAT25qKGvBuDNM/story.html
26. Barber, M. (2008). What is the "Gay Agenda" in America? *Mass Resistance.* Retrieved fromhttps://www.massresistance.org/docs/gen/08a/barber_gayagenda.html
27. Serrano, A. (2006). Evangelical Quits After Gay Sex Scandal. *CBS News.* Retrieved fromttps://www.cbsnews.com/news/evangelical-quits-after-gay-sex-scandal/
28. Jones, M. W. (2018). Jim and Tammy Faye Bakker: A Scandal of the Self. *Weekly Standard.* Retrieved from https://www.weeklystandard.com/martyn-wendell-jones/jim-and-tammy-faye-bakker-a-scandal-of-the-self
29. The Associated Press. (2006). Inmate Testifies Why He Killed Molester Priest. *New York Times.* Retrieved from https://www.nytimes.com/2006/01/24/us/inmate-testifies-why-he-killed-molester-priest.html
30. Magida, A. J. (2009). *The Rabbi and the Hit Man: A True Tale of Murder, Passion, and Shattered Faith.* New York, NY: Harper Collins.
31. Kurkjian, S. & Cullen, K. (2002). Grand jury indicts Shanley, rape of four boys. *The Boston Globe.* Retrieved from http://graphics.boston.com/globe/spotlight/abuse/stories2/062102_shanley.htm
32. Fox News. (2017). Sheikh Omar Abdel-Rahman, linked to 1993 World Trade Center attack, has Died. *Fox News.* Retrieved from https://www.foxnews.com/us/sheikh-omar-abdel-rahman-linked-to-1993-world-trade-center-attack-has-died

33. Jimmy Swaggart. (1988). *BBC News*. Retrieved from http://news.bbc.co.uk/onthisday/hi/dates/stories/february/21/newsid_2565000/2565197.st m
34. Confederate Flag. (n.d.). *Dixie Outfitters*. Retrieved from https://dixieoutfitters.com/category/in-the-news/controversy-over-confederate flag/outrage-over-confederate-flag/
35. Confederate Monuments. (2017). *American Historical Association*. Retrieved from https://www.historians.org/news-and-advocacy/statements-and-resolutions-of- support-and-protest/aha-statement-on-confederate-monuments
36. Estepa, J. (2017). House Minority Leader Nancy Pelosi calls for removal of Confederate statues from Capitol. *USA Today*. Retrieved from https://www.usatoday.com/story/news/politics/onpolitics/2017/08/17/house-minority-leader-nancy-pelosi-calls-for-removal-of-confederate-statues-capitol/576498001/
37. Khruschchev in America. (n.d.) Retrieved from https://archive.org/stream/khrushchevinamer006997mbp/khrushchevinamer006997mbp_djvu.txt
38. Tuttle, I. (2017). Bernie Sanders, Theocrat. *National Review*. Retrieved from https://www.nationalreview.com/2017/06/bernie-sanders-russell-vought-tim-farron-religious-views/
39. Hallowell, B. (2017). Report: Public School Teacher Fired After Giving Student a Copy of the Bible Scores Major Victory. *Faith Wire*. Retrieved from https://www.faithwire.com/2017/05/12/report-public-school-teacher-fired-after- giving-
40. Associated Press. (2016). Football coach fired for postgame prayer takes action against school. *CBS News*. Retrieved from

https://www.cbsnews.com/news/washington-football-coach-fired-for-post-game-prayer-takes-action-against-school/
41. Cochran v. City of Atlanta – Alliance Defending Freedom. Retrieved from www.adfmedia.org/News/PRDetail/9520
42. Silva, C. (2016). Who Is Monifa Sterling? Bible And Religious Freedom Debated By Military Court After Marine Discharged For Sharing Scripture. *IB Times*. Retrieved from https://www.ibtimes.com/whrelo-monifa-sterling-bible-religious-freedom-debated-militarycourt-after-marine-2361210
43. Smith, C. (2018). California Bill AB 2943 and What It Means for Religious Freedom. *Approaching Justice*. Retrieved from https://approachingjustice.net/2018/04/21/california-bill-ab-2943-and-what-it-means- for-religious-freedom/
44. Bernstein, R. (1988). In Dispute on Bias, Stanford Is Likely To Alter Western Culture Program. *The New York Times*. Retrieved from https://www.nytimes.com/1988/01/19/us/in-dispute-on-bias-stanford-is-likely-to-alter-western-culture-program.html

Chapter Three

45. America No Longer a Christian Nation. (2014). YouTube clip retrieved from https://www.youtube.com/watch?v=zOOrSAbU9z8
46. Christian Statistic/ These facts may surprise you. Retrieved from www.rotw.com/
47. Survey: White evangelicals Retrieved from https://religionnews.com

48. Richard Nixon. (2017). National Archives. Retrieved from https://www.archives.gov/education/lessons/watergate-constitution
49. Gerald Ford. (n. d.) Ford Library & Museum. Retrieved from https://www.fordlibrarymuseum.gov/library/speeches/740060.asp
50. Milligan, S. (2018). Building a Legacy: Former President Jimmy Carter talks of his life's work on affordable housing and the future of public service. *US News*. Retrieved from https://www.usnews.com/news/the-report/articles/2018-08-31/jimmy-carter-on-affordable-housing-and-public-service
51. Ronald Reagan. (2018). Encyclopedia Britannica. Retrieved from https://www.britannica.com/biography/Ronald-Reagan
52. Ronald Reagan Funeral Service. (2004). *C-Span*. Retrieved from https://www.c-span.org/video/?182165-1/ronald-reagan-funeral-service
53. Keneally, M. (2017). Multiple women accuse former President George HW Bush of Inappropriate grabbing. *ABC News*. Retrieved from https://abcnews.go.com/US/multiple-women-accuse-president-george-hw-bush-inappropriate/story?id=51204025
54. Merida, K. (1998). It's Come To This: A Nickname That's Proven Hard to Slip. Washington.Post. Retrieved from http://www.washingtonpost.com/wp-zsrv/politics/special/clinton/stories/slick122098.htm
55. Gerth, J. & Engleberg, S. (1993). U.S. Investigating Clinton's Links to Arkansas S.& L. *The New York Times*. Retrieved from https://www.nytimes.com/1993/11/02/us/us-investigating-clinton-s-links-to-arkansas-s-l.html
56. Berman, S. (2017). We owe a huge apology to Juanita Broaddrick, Paula Jones and Kathleen Willey.

NOQ Report. Retrieved fromhttps://noqreport.com/2017/11/14/owe-huge-apology-juanita-broaddrick-paula-jones-kathleen-willey/

57. Glass, A. (2018). Clinton's Senate impeachment end, Feb. 12, 1999. *Politico.* Retrieved from https://www.politico.com/story/2018/02/12/this-day-in-politics-feb-12-1999-401098
58. Chretien, C. (2016). FLASHBACK: Bill Clinton on veto of partial-birth abortion: 'Hillary and I prayed about it. *Life Site News.* Retrieved from https://www.lifesitenews.com/pulse/bill-clinton-i-vetoed-partial-birth-abortion-ban-because-hillary-and-i-pray
59. Sanger, D. E. (1994). Clinton Approves a Plan to Give Aid to North Koreans. *New York Times.*Retrieved from https://www.nytimes.com/1994/10/19/world/clinton-approves-a-plan-to-give-aid-to-north-koreans.html
60. George W. Bush. (n.d.) On The Issues. Retrieved from http://issues2000.org/2004/George_W__Bush_Abortion.htm
61. Barack Obama. (n.d.) *Encyclopedia of World Biography.* Retrieved from https://www.notablebiographies.com/news/Li-Ou/Obama-Barack.html
62. Root, W. A. (2013). Ghost of Columbia – Part II: Legendary Columbia Professor Never Heard of Obama. *The Blaze.* Retrieved fromhttps://www.theblaze.com/contributions/ghost-of-columbia-part-ii-legendary-columbia-professor-never-heard-of-obama
63. Hayward, J. (2017). 18 Major Scandals in Obama's 'Scandal-Free' Presidency. *Breitbart.* Retrieved from https://www.breitbart.com/politics/2017/01/02/18-major-scandals-obama-presidency/

64. Gertz, B. (2015). Obama secretly backing Muslim Brotherhood. Washington Times. Retrieved from https://www.washingtontimes.com/news/2015/jun/3/inside-the-ring-muslim-brotherhood-has-obamas-secr/
65. Beck, G. (2015). Obama administration used your tax dollars in failed attempt to unseat Benjamin Netanyahu. *Glenn Beck.* Retrieved from https://www.glennbeck.com/2015/03/18/obama-administration-used-your-tax-dollars-in-failed-attempt-to-unseat-benjamin-netanyahu/
66. Whitehead, J. W. (2015). The Deep State: The Unelected Shadow Government Is Here to Stay. *The Rutherford Institute.* Retrieved from https://www.rutherford.org/publications_resources/john_whiteheads_commentary/the_deep_state_the_unelected_shadow_government_is_here_to_stay
67. Globalism. (2018). *Merriam-Webster*. Retrieved from https://www.merriam-webster.com/dictionary/globalism
68. Louis T. McFadden Speech. (1932). *SCRIBD*. Retrieved fromhttps://www.scribd.com/doc/16502353/Congressional-Record-June-10-1932-Louis-T-McFadden
69. Same Sex Marriages. (2014). Retrieved from https://www.supremecourt.gov/opinions/14pdf/14-556_3204.pdf
70. First Amendment and Religion. (n.d.) *US Courts*. Retrieved from http://www.uscourts.gov/educational-resources/educational-activities/first-amendment-and-religion
71. Engel v. Vitale. (1962). *Digital History*. Retrieved from http://www.digitalhistory.uh.edu/disp_textbook.cfm?smtID=3&psid=1197

72. Waggoner, M. D. (2012). When the Court Took on Prayer and the Bible in Public Schools. *Religion & Politics*. Retrieved from https://religionandpolitics.org/2012/06/25/when-the-court-took-on-prayer-the-bible-and-public-schools/
73. McCullough, S. R. (2018). School District of Abington Township v. Schempp. *Encyclopedia Britannica*. Retrieved from https://www.britannica.com/topic/School-District-of-Abington-Township-v-Schempp
74. Stone v. Graham (1980). *Find Law*. Retrieved from https://caselaw.findlaw.com/us-supreme-court/449/39.html
75. Lee v. Weisman. (1992). *Find Law*. Retrieved from https://caselaw.findlaw.com/us-supreme-court/505/577.html
76. Santa Fe Independent School District v. Doe. (2000). *Find Law*. Retrieved from https://caselaw.findlaw.com/us-supreme-court/530/290.html
77. Marshall, R. (2014). School Life in the 1960s. *Reading Through History*. Retrieved from http://readingthroughhistory.com/2014/06/20/1960s-schools/
78. Unborn Victims of Violence Act of 2004. (2004). *Government Publishing Office*. Retrieved from https://www.gpo.gov/fdsys/pkg/PLAW-108publ212/pdf/PLAW-108publ212.pdf
79. Pollack, H. (2014). Alcohol linked to more homicides in US than any other substance. *NewHaven Register*. Retrieved from https://www.nhregister.com/connecticut/article/Alcohol-linked-to-more-homicides-in- US-than-any-11378638.php

Chapter Four

80. The History of Gun Control. (2018). *The Firearms Forum.* Retrieved from https://www.thefirearmsforum.com/threads/the-history-of-gun-control.1799 Mitchell, 81. 7 Startling Facts: Retreived from An U... https://churchleaders.com
81. 2017 California wildfires –Retrieved from https://en.wikipedia.org/wiki/2017_California_wildfires
82. Terrorism in America. (2018). *New America.* Retrieved from https://www.newamerica.org/in-depth/terrorism-in-america/part-i-overview-terrorism-cases-2001-today/
83. Morton, V. & LeBlanc, J. (2015). Husband-wife team, Syed Farook and Tashfeen Malik, identified as San Bernardino killers. *Washington Times.* Retrieved from https://www.washingtontimes.com/news/2015/dec/2/syed-farook-identified-san- bernardino-shooting-sus/
84. Ray, M. (2018). Orlando shooting of 2016. *Encyclopedia Britannica.* Retrieved from https://www.britannica.com/event/Orlando-shooting-of-201686. Bacon, J. (2016).
85. Eleven hurt, suspect killed in 'terrifying' Ohio State attack. USA Today. Retrieved fromhttps://www.usatoday.com/story/news/nation/2016/11/28/ohio-state-reports-active-shooter-columbus-campus/94540050/
86. Darrah, N. (2017). NYC terror attack leaves 8 dead, several injured; suspect's notes pledged ISIS Loyalty. *Fox News.* Retrieved from https://www.foxnews.com/us/nyc-terror-attack-leaves-8-dead-several-injured-suspects-notes-pledged-isis-loyalty

87. Starr, P. (2017). FBI: 33,000 Criminal Gangs, 1.4 Million Members Active in U.S. *Breitbart.* Retrieved from https://www.breitbart.com/national-security/2017/06/15/fbi-33000-criminal-gangs-1-4-million-members-active-in-u-s/
88. Crime Increase in 2016. (2016). *Major Cities Chiefs Association.* Retrieved from https://www.majorcitieschiefs.com/pdf/news/mcca_violent_crime_data_midyear_20162015.pdf

Who is Don Ledbetter?

Dr. Don Ledbetter was born in Anniston, Alabama. He and his wife, Linda, have two sons, Steve and Stan, two precious daughter-in-law's, Carolyn and Angela, and three grandchildren, Alysha, Zachary, and Hannah.

Don served as senior pastor of four churches, two in Alabama, and two in Georgia. After his seventeen-year pastoral ministry, he entered vocational evangelism. Since entering evangelism, he has conducted numerous revivals and evangelism crusades across America. He has served two terms as president of the Georgia Baptist Evangelist. He has preached for the Florida, Georgia, and Tennessee Baptist State Conventions. He is a published author and a gifted artist. His artwork is on display across America.

He has authored: Deacon Relationship through the Body of Christ
Satan, Deception, and Scriptural Misconceptions
Does God Consider All "Marriages," Marriages?

Each of these books are available from Amazon or in 25,000 bookstores across America.

Dr. Ledbetter is also an excellent teacher. He has conducted Deacon Retreats, Marriage Retreats, and Sunday

School Seminars across America. For four consecutive years, he has lectured at the New Orleans Seminary Campus in Atlanta on the subject, "What an Evangelist Wished Every Pastor Knew about Revival."

He graduated from the Bible College of Florida and he has earned a Doctor of Ministry Degree from Luther Rice College & Seminary.

Dr. Ledbetter can be reached at:
P.O. Box 689
Fayetteville, Georgia 30214